Martial Thoughts

by

Edgardo Perez

Edited
by
Erin Mulder

For my wonderful family that always manages
to put up with all my nonsense. Life is precious,
with them in my life it has been pure joy.
Thank you, Liz, Ronni and Rico.

"The warrior is not one who fights, for no one has the right to take another life. The warrior, for us, is someone who sacrifices himself for the good of others. His task is to take care of the elderly, the defenseless, those who cannot provide for themselves, and above all, the children, the future of humanity."

-Sitting Bull
Chief and Warrior of the Lakota Nation

The martial arts have been a strong part of my life, having begun my formal training at age 14. Now, over 40 years later, I have had the privilege of meeting, training with and teaching some extraordinary martial artists. Although I consider myself an extremely eclectic trainer, I'll use anything that works and I am notorious for adding new "twists" to my existing systems, I'm still a traditionalist in the philosophical aspects of it. I'm old fashioned and believe that the martial arts should still be used as a way of self-improvement, not just physically but mentally and psychologically as well. It's not just about the fight, and, although this is the core and root of it, that is not all that there is.

On the day you depart from this World, will others say that it is a better place now than when you arrived? What do you think? I pose this question to my students all the time and encourage them to do their part, no matter how small it may seem.
I can spend my life training fighters but I'd rather train defenders, I can train you to survive but I'd rather train you to win. To survive is not the same thing as winning and losing without learning is the only true loss.

In schools our children are taught formal education and reminded daily that they should conform to the norms that society has created for them. They are not taught the reality of life when they are constantly bombarded with reminders that no matter what they do, it's good enough, that it doesn't matter if they came in 5th place, they are all still winners. This is the same as learning a few martial arts techniques and your instructor telling you how good you are only to get punched in the face after your first fight and waking up five minutes later. Life is the perfect Dojo and it does not pull any punches, get ready.

The following words are based on random conversations that I have had with my students at one time or another in the past twenty-five years. They are my words based on my humble opinions and some stories associated with them. In red I have added words and quotes from some great past leaders & warriors as well as current mentors related in some way to the topic. It is my hope that these words will also help encourage you on your warrior's path and that you will draw something useful from my experience.

Be Strong, Be Thankful, Be of Service......and always watch your six.

Edgardo Perez,
W. Commander (Police ret.)
Maestro de Guazábara

THE WARRIORS PATH

THINK LIKE A WARRIOR

THE WARRIOR WITHIN

On a small island, a storm rages and batters its coast, powerful winds

force trees to fight for survival as they attempt to remain anchored to the earth. In the midst of the storm, a building can be found standing tall in defiance of the weather, a light at the top proudly displaying its duty to others.

Offshore, a small ship fights for its own survival as the wind and water push it to its limits.

In the distance, the light from the building is seen, the captain uses the light to help him navigate his way to the shore, toward safety.

Pushing to the back of his mind all the dangers that the storm possesses, the captain focuses on the light, all the things that could happen if the storm wins this battle must be ignored, he will not allow himself to lose focus, the light is the target. The light has now become an important means of survival for the captain, a way for him to find safe harbor.

The ship fights the captain, it wants to go with the storm, flow into the abyss and take the captain along. But he is a warrior, he refuses to allow the ship to have its way, he refuses to capitulate to the storm. The light, if he focuses on the light, will point the way, he will make it, he will survive, he will win.

On shore the small tower stands tall with its beacon at the top, its sole existence is to guide those that are lost, those that are trying to survive. The Lighthouse, managed by The Warrior Within, will bring the captain home.

In this short story both the ship's Captain and the lighthouse Keeper are warriors. One is on a journey of survival and the other is there as the guide. Which one are you? In life you will find times that you will be both, in the ship and in the lighthouse, fighting to survive the storm or guiding others.

The body, like the lighthouse, must be made strong, powerful and resistant to attack, only then can you be there for others, only then can you help guide others to safety, shelter and defend those in need.

Roger, a colleague of mine, someone who in the past I have done youth programs with, is easily one of the gentlest human beings I have ever met. This amazing human being makes himself available 24 hours a day so that he can answer the suicide hotline and speak with people who are on the verge of giving up and ending their lives. We may never know how many lives he has saved but the amazing part about this human lighthouse is that he doesn't focus on that, as soon as he saves one life he immediately focuses on the other. Although he may not think of himself as a badass, I will always think of him that way.

"Whoever saves one life, save the world entire."

-Oskar Schindler

WHAT IS THE WARRIOR WAY?

Learning to live the Warrior Way is a journey of constant training and development of the body and mind. The warrior who is living in the Way remains always prepared for confrontation, for defense and yes...for death. Many think that training in the martial arts is living in the Way...wrong. Training in the martial arts can be one aspect of that but it is not a necessary component. I have met many who have never trained in any type of fighting arts but are living the Warrior Way and sadly, I have met the opposite.

The warrior who lives and follows the Way does so by following a  moral code or guideline, is constantly training his/her mind for survival and defense, serves those in need and always stands ready to face the "storm", especially in times of peace. They remain in a state of constant growth, everyday trying to be better than they were yesterday, not just physically but mentally as well.

Those who live in the Way understand that the mind can also be flawed. We may suffer from depression, anxiety and low self-esteem but we also need to understand that to think and be this way is OK and that those issues are a part of life. It doesn't make us victims or special, it simply reminds us that we are alive and that we may have to fight harder than others to achieve our personal goals. As long as we know this, we push past the obstacles and force ourselves to move on, to persevere and to do what others will not. Why? Because as a warrior, it is understood that you will not stop until there is nothing left, that even when the odds are against you and all hope is lost, those who live by this creed know that death is a part of life and they will always live their lives in such a way that when death finally does come to claim them, it arrives with back up.

A hero of mine, Major League Baseball Hall of Fame member, Roberto Clemente would say, *"If you have a chance to accomplish something that will make things better for people coming behind you, and you don't do that, you are wasting your time on this Earth."* Sadly,

he lost his life on December 31, 1972, while in route to deliver aid to earthquake victims in Nicaragua. He could have easily been at home with his family preparing for a fun New Year's celebration, but his thoughts were on those that needed help and he chose to be of service to those in need. He was a true warrior and an inspiration to many.

YOU'RE NOT A VICTIM!

It seems to me that in today's day and age, we like to think of victims as heroes, as people we should look up to and venerate, but in actuality, that's not the case. We think of them as heroes because they survived, overcame tragedy and somehow, through personal fortitude, came out on top and were able to share their story.

Some people will say, "look at him/her, aren't they amazing?" We focus on the victim, failing to look at them as more than what they truly are, survivors. Very little can inspire anyone more than the story of someone who has encountered a tragedy that would have broken most people, but refuses to remain or thought of as a victim. The survivors of the Boston Marathon bombing in April of 2013 were a great example, many refused to surrender to that day, they were not going to allow those who had chosen to do them harm to win the fight, they were not victims. How about all our warriors who return from combat with injuries both visible and invisible? I look at them with such a high level of admiration, not because of the injury, but because of the power within them that refuses to allow their personal pain to dominate their existence. These men and women are no one's victims, and when they share those events, they do so as survivors and winners.

When you read these stories, and there are a lot of them out there, you may tend to become empathetic toward the storyteller and see them as a victim, don't! That is just the beginning of the story. This, in my opinion, is what glorifies victimhood, the failure of seeing the big picture, of not understanding that the story is incomplete. For the survivor, the tragedy is just the first chapter.

There is no strength in being a victim! That can happen to anyone and no one wants that. Your strength comes from never giving up, refusing to surrender and knowing that you're the hero of the story, the survivor. Morihei Ueshiba, Samurai and founder of Aikido, would say *"The samurai is the first to suffer anxiety for human society, and he is the last to seek personal pleasure."*

Think of Marcus Latrell, The Lone Survivor. Imagine the heartache of losing all your comrades. Through pain and suffering he fights on, the battle never ends, the scars may not be visible but they are definitely there.

Do not seek to win the sympathy of others by displaying your pain the way a peacock displays its feathers, you're better than that.

"I died on that mountain. There is no question. A part of me will forever be upon that mountain. Dead. That's my brother's mountain. If there's a part of me that lives, it's because of my brother's. Because of them I am still alive, and I could never forget, that no matter how much it hurts, how dark it gets, or how far you fall, you are never out of the fight."

-Marcus Luttrell
Navy Seal
Lone Survivor

MY EGO, MY ENEMY

It is important to identify your enemies, know who they are, what they represent and how you can defeat them.

One of the greatest enemies that we have and that we all share, no one is immune, is our ego. When you are learning something new, it's your

ego that may step in and say things to you like, "you don't need to do that" or "what's the point?" The ego will impede your training, force your mind to shut down and close. The fact is, your mind should be open and constantly looking for ways to improve your skills.

"I don't need to train, when the time comes, I'll be ready". You may or may not have heard these words spoken by those who refuse to train or work hard to improve their skills. These individuals are often minimalists, the ones who do as little as possible but feel entitled to receive the greatest rewards. Allowing their ego to dictate their tactics, they will often fall short of their goals and blame others for it. Recognize when you've fallen onto this negative way of thinking and do whatever you can to find your way out. Outside influences will always pull you in different directions affecting your mood and behavior, avoid this at all cost, this is not for you!

Your mental door is either open or closed, a person with a fixed mindset has made the decision that there's nothing worth learning and that they have managed to obtain all the necessary skills and knowledge needed to achieve their goals. On the opposite side of that, the Alpha warrior will always maintain a growth mindset, for them, the "door" is always open. They are like a sponge, focused and absorbing knowledge and information, absolutely everything that will help them rise to their full potential and meet the objective.

When the mind is open and constantly searching, knowledge can be found everywhere. Keep an open, growth mindset and a day will never pass without improvement.

"Live as if you were to die tomorrow. Learn as if you were to live forever."-Mahatma Gandhi

<u>The Viking Prayer</u>

"Lo, there do I see my father.

Lo, there do I see my mother,

and my sisters, and my brothers.

Lo, there do I see the line of my people,

Back to the beginning!

Lo, they do call to me.

They bid me take my place among them,

In the halls of Valhalla!

Where the brave may live forever!

The 13th Warrior
1999 Film adapted from the book
Eaters of The Dead by Michael Crichton

A WARRIOR'S HEART

 There is a fundamental joy in teaching the martial arts and watching the fledgling student go from learning the very basics to becoming confident in their skills. I spend most of the time searching for different ways to help the student grasp the knowledge and perform the techniques being taught. Everyone is different and learns at their own pace, it's the instructor's job to find the best way. Some will learn quickly and only after a few attempts will appear to have a fundamental understanding, I am grateful for them. Others will have a very hard time and will struggle to understand the most basic concepts. I am grateful for them as well, it's these students that will help me become a better coach and teacher. The students that struggle will be the ones that force me to try alternative ways of teaching and keep searching until they begin to understand.

A good instructor can teach you the ways of the martial arts but they cannot make you good, they cannot make you master the techniques, only the student can do that, they are inevitably their own teachers, the instructor is merely the guide that points the way"

Those who show up at my front door without training, can soon learn to obtain the skills needed to defend themselves, skill can always be taught but the heart is the main ingredient. The student-warrior must

18

absolutely have heart. Heart is NOT what starts you on your journey, it's what keeps you there and forces you to keep going even when everything or everyone else is telling you to stop.

I'm a huge fan of Sylvester Stallone's *Rocky*. What made Rocky so formidable was his inability to quit, he just would not stay down. His boxing career showed that he wasn't the most skilled fighter, didn't have much style and was thought of as a Southpaw puncher, most boxing coaches didn't want anything to do with him. Chance gave him an opportunity that would never be repeated. Rocky didn't care to win the fight, he merely wanted to last longer against the champion than any previous opponent ever had. He pushed himself harder and trained better than he ever had before. Heart

gave him the determination and will power to stay in the ring when even his manager wanted to throw in the towel. Why do I love that movie so much? How can you not!? He just wouldn't stay down!

The day you wrap that black belt around your waist, or get down to your ideal weight or finally accomplish that goal you've been working toward, the minute you accomplish these great things for the first time, you know that you didn't do it for someone else or because you had the right amount of skill or even because you had a good coach/teacher/mentor, you did it because you had a Warrior's Heart.

"A lion sleeps in the heart of every brave man."
Turkish Proverb

GUAZÁBARA RULES

1. Defend the tribe, defend the people.

2. Be Humble in your acts and deeds.

3. Honor above all things, even Loyalty.

4. Your Training and Skills should be treated with respect, do not abuse what you have learned.

5. Always stand against evil or share in the offense.

6. Give freely, help those in need but do so with humility.

7. Know your enemy.

8. Always give respect and demand it of yourself.

9. Be of Service.

Daca Guazábara, Daca Naboria Yaya

CODE OF THE WARRIOR LEADER
Trust Your Instincts

For thousands of years our instincts have warned us and kept us aware of dangers that were present. Today, we like to use such names as a hunch, gut feeling or women's intuition. Our instincts, like our muscles, need to be trained and worked so that they can grow and remain strong. During peacetime, a warrior is reminded to

always keep his sword sharp, in other words, keep your body strong and your mind always ready.

When we live in times of peace, some choose to ignore and allow their warrior skills to atrophy and become useless, that is not the warrior way. Keep your mind on point, this starts by listening and learning to trust what our inner voice is telling us.

Engage your Awareness

Awareness is 70% of your self-defense. Becoming aware of danger before it happens will better prepare you for a proper response. In many cases you may be able to totally avoid a dangerous situation. Stay in the moment and open your mind and eyes to see that which others do not. Become a student of human nature and learn to study people, as you train this ability you will begin to notice subtle changes in behaviors that may be contrary to your current environment, somethings not right!

22

In my early years of undercover narcotics work, the target offender would often want to meet me in a crowded place such as a bar or restaurant. The team and I would often get to the meet location first so that I could get situated and allow them time to find places where they would have the best visibility. It was important for us to observe the environment, escape routes and people present. If by chance, the target offender arrived at the meeting location first, then I would make it a point, upon entry, of not becoming completely focused on him/her, but would first do a quick scan of the surroundings to see if there was someone else there that was in "play" but not part of the original plan, counter surveillance was always a possibility and would happen often.

"No people have a better use of their 5 senses than the children of the wilderness. We could smell as well as hear and see. We could feel and taste as well as we could see and hear. Nowhere has the memory been more fully developed than in the wildlife."

-Dr. Charles Eastman (Ohiyesa)
Native American of the Santee Dakota People
Author & Physician

Have a Plan

The time to plan is not when the incident is occurring. Come up with different scenarios and possible encounters, then begin to think of how you would respond to them. Continuously think on those plans, what your response would be and possible escapes if the situation calls for that. This will increase your response time and raise your survival rate considerably. Recently I read a book by John C.

Maxwell, "How Successful People Think". In this book, which I would highly recommend reading, the author speaks about the old saying, *"crossing that bridge when we come to it"*. This discussion was part of a bigger subject that he was referencing that had to do with seeing the bigger picture. I saw it additionally as not being properly prepared for conflict, this is something that I hear often by those who feel that training is unnecessary and assume that when the moment of conflict arrives, they, the untrained and untested, will be ready. They...will...not! (I'll revisit this subject in further detail later.)

"A good plan violently executed now is better than a perfect plan executed next week."

-General George Patton

Know the Ways of Others

Miyamoto Musashi (宮本 武蔵, 12 March 1584–13 June 1645), the famous Japanese samurai who never lost a duel would say, "know the ways of others". He would often speak of the importance of stepping out of what is known and comfortable and learn new things, study different fighting methods and warriors of all cultures. To beat your opponent, you must learn their ways.

I have never stopped training or trying to learn different styles. Even though Korean Hapkido is my chosen martial system, it is not the style of Hapkido I started training in over forty years ago. My hybrid version contains aspects of Shaolin Chin-na Fa, Filipino Escrima, Jeet Kune Do, Jiu-Jitsu and especially Guazábara.

If you train in the martial arts and are not proficient in ALL areas of it, then you're not proficient, it's that simple. If you lack skill in ground combatives or weapons, find someone who's skill surpasses your own, then train.

Whenever a Warrior decides to go do something, he must go all the way. No matter what he does, he must know first why he is doing it, and then he must proceed with his actions without having doubt or remorse about them. -Carlos Castenada, *The Journey to Ixtla*

Carlson Gracie, Jr. and Mark Daley demonstrating the Rear Naked Choke during a seminar at the Defense Training Institute in 2010. This seminar was one of several that we would host combining ground fundamentals to our martial arts program.

Do not Focus on the Outcome...DO IT!

Too much thought is placed on negative possibilities when you're trying something new, especially the thought of failure. Do not focus on what could happen, focus simply on doing your best!

Some of our greatest heroes and warriors have lost more times than they've won but continued to persevere because they knew what they were fighting for and that there was no losing, there was only winning and learning.

Focus on the possibilities for success, not the potential for failure.

Napoleon Hill

Acquire Empathy

Learn to put yourself in another's place, this will help you to better understand what they are going through and how their thinking may differ from yours. Not everyone has walked the same path as you and all our individual stories have helped to shape and guide us. Imagine yourself walking in another's shoes, the world may seem different from their vantage point.

This is the nature of war; by protecting others, you save yourself. If you only think of yourself, you'll only destroy yourself. -Seven Samurai (1954)

Maintain a Warrior Presence

Always think of yourself as the leading authority, the alpha! Present yourself with confidence. Stand straight, be cognizant of your personal appearance, stay focused and aware, listen intently and speak plainly. Let them feel your power and your intensity, let it flow from you like a raging river.

Think of yourself as always about to go into battle. Everything depends on your frame of mind and how you look at the world. A shift of perspective can transform you from a passive and confused mercenary into a motivated and creative fighter. -Excerpt from the 33 Strategies of War by Robert Green

Never Quit!

There may come a time when you may feel that you cannot go one more day, that you are no longer interested in completing your mission, you're tired, mentally and physically. Don't stop. Remember and focus on what started you on this current path.

Your personal mission can be a goal that you've set for yourself or a project that you promised yourself you would complete. Never allow yourself to be defeated, you can falter, fall, stumble or just plain slow down, but you will never stop. Another factor that you need to focus on is the small wins that, although they feel great, are only a part of the goal. Winning the majority of the battles will lead to victory in war but not if you're so caught up with patting yourself on the back for the small win and you lose sight of the big picture. The day you fulfill the mission objective is the day you plan your tactics for the next battle, it never ends, you never stop, you never quit.

"Never quit, you have to resist to the utmost, till you drop, like a Samurai." -Carlson Gracie, Sr.

Develop a Sense of Malice

Think like your enemy. Don't be the enemy, train your mind to THINK like them. What would your opponent do? How would they react in a variety of situations? Don't allow your personal moral compass to dictate your thoughts, not this time. Play the game of placing yourself in those positions and see what you would do. This particular skill set will help you become a student of human nature and see things from angles that you would normally ignore, this additionally will help you prepare a proper response.

This is paramount for an undercover officer, don't think like a cop, place yourself in the role of the criminal. For the undercover officer, this is different than what an actor would do, there are no do-overs, no lines to memorize and your life is in constant jeopardy.

If you want to hunt the Wolf, you must think like one and if you think like them, you'll be better prepared to anticipate their actions.

"To know your enemy, you must become your enemy."

-Sun Tzu

Inspire Others

Your very presence should be an inspiration to others. What you say matters little in comparison to what you do. Make yourself the example and let your actions do the talking. Words are nice but your actions are what will drive others to achieve a higher level. Many of you reading this have worked for individuals who "talk a good game" but never seem to be willing to get their hands dirty and do the "sweat labor" required to accomplish the work.

My Dad was my hero, he never shared a lot of knowledge or used great words with my brothers and sister but he constantly demonstrated what was required to get things done. His work ethic was something that as I got older, I learned to appreciate more and more. He would take his breaks but only after all the work was done. I never heard him complain about his job, even though it was back breaking work, he persevered and would even take any overtime that was offered him, anything that would help him take care of his family. His actions served as our inspiration. Our continuous drive to be the best at whatever we did is a direct relation to the man who put us on our path.

Take Ownership

We've all worked with and for people who, when things don't go as planned, are quick to blame someone or find an excuse. These are the fair-weather leaders, there usually the ones that have risen to their highest level of incompetence and have yet to admit that they are in over their heads. Many will jump into the position of leadership because it pays better or for status but fail to understand that the team, organization or people pay the price. Many (most) of our politicians fall into this category.

Good or bad, anything that occurs under your watch is your responsibility, whether you were completely made aware of all the details or not. No one forced you into this position, as a leader, it all ends with you, you are responsible so don't hide from it, take responsibility, share the credit and take ownership.

"Total responsibility for failure is a difficult thing to accept, and taking ownership when things go wrong requires extraordinary humility and courage. But doing just that is an absolute necessity to learning, growing as a leader, and improving a team's performance."

-Jocko Willink, Navy Seal

Be of Service

The true meaning of the word Samurai is "one who serves". It's not just about being in the service of their lord but also in the service of the people. To know that they existed to serve and be there for others was the highest honor.

The mission and part of the motto of most law enforcement agencies is to "Serve and Protect", to protect those in need and serve their communities. As I had mentioned earlier, it is my belief that being a fighter does not make you a warrior, you must also serve. Heavyweight Champion of the World Mohammed Ali was a great fighter but he did not become a warrior until he learned the value of service.

"Service to others is the rent you pay for your room here on Earth". - Mohammed Ali

Honor Above All

I do not put this last because it is the least concern, it is placed in the last position in the hopes that it will be remembered the best. We often remember the last thing we hear, see or read.

Your honor and integrity must shine like a beacon so that others can feel it. We are not monks or holy men; many will falter and do the wrong thing but a person of honor will always strive to find the path that leads back to the honorable way.

In your life, you will meet a wide variety of people. Both poor and rich alike have the ability to be honorable, it is not directly related to economic status. You must look beyond the obvious and "see" into the soul of the person.

"It isn't position which lends men distinction, but men who enhance positions". -Leonidas, Agiad King and Leader of the Spartans

Rocky's Speech to His Son

"The world ain't all sunshine and rainbows. It is a very mean and nasty place and it will beat you to your knees and keep you there permanently if you let it. You, me, or nobody is gonna hit as hard as life. But it ain't how hard you hit; it's about how hard you can get hit, and keep moving forward. How much you can take, and keep moving forward. That's how winning is done. Now, if you know what you're worth, then go out and get what you're worth. But you gotta be willing to take the hit, and not pointing fingers saying you ain't where you are because of him, or her, or anybody. Cowards do that and that ain't you. You're better than that!" - Rocky Balboa

Sylvester Stallone's *Rocky Balboa*

THE ESSENCE OF WARRIORHOOD

What does it mean to be a warrior and why is it more than just about fighting. We've all heard the term "Warrior" bantered around and used along with such words as, spiritual warrior, financial warrior, business warrior, etc. But none of these are true warriors. A warrior, by its true definition, is a person, from any walk of life, who is in the service of others, lives by a code of conduct

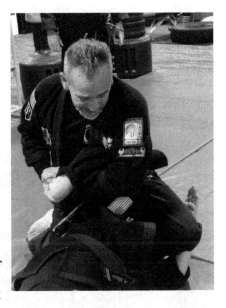

and is always ready to shield and protect the weak. Ancient warriors protected their people, they were their hunters, their enforcers, their defenders and guardians. They insured the survival of the tribe. This, in the modern day, has not changed. The people are still protected by warriors. Today they come in all sizes and shapes, from all walks of life. You are no longer born into a warrior cast, today, you make the choice. When the common man or woman chooses to train, to defend another, to help them in their time of need, you have chosen the warrior's path. So you see, it's all about choice.

As I mentioned earlier, it is my belief that the necessary ingredients for warriorhood is to be prepared to stand in defense of others, continuously guided by a code of conduct and in service to others. Without these component's, one might be a good person, but that does

33

not make you a warrior. You can also be an extremely talented fighter but that also does not qualify you.

Our world needs warriors, we're desperate for them, especially now. We need them in positions of leadership and authority, as guides and protectors, in all aspects of life.

If you're reading this then I have to believe that you're trying to feed  your warrior spirit, why else would you be reading the words of this old warrior. You are on the right path, don't second guess yourself, please. Start by accomplishing small things and make them wins, those wins will be the small victories that will push you forward into the final battle. Be the warrior that God meant for you to be, be there for others, there are many who are waitng and depending on you.

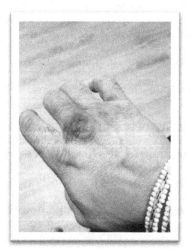

Blessed be the Lord my Rock who trains my hands for war, and my fingers for battle.

-Psalm 144.11

THINK LIKE A WARRIOR

Who Dares, Wins.
Who Sweats, Wins
Who Plans, Wins.
-British Special Air Service
(SAS)

STAND FAST

The term "Stand Fast" is often used by military and police personnel to let others know to be alert and ready to move. It's a reminder to put yourself in Cooper's Condition Orange (we will talk more about this later) by becoming hyper focused and engaged.

We all have a tendency to relax when we are in situations that are considered routine. Sometimes it's important to stop what you're doing and perform a quick mental recon of your area and environment.

Well known actor and student of martial discipline, Scott Glenn, understands the need to keep the body strong and ready for combat. In a January 2016 interview with GQ Magazine, the interviewer asked: "So, the key to looking like you when you're 75 is never stop being a badass." Glenn: *"Well, I don't like the word 'badass' because I train with guys up in Idaho from SEAL Team 6. And my son-in-law—I think of him as my son—has been a SEAL for most of his adult life. So, I know what badass really is. It's like when you see MMA guys, you know, out on the mats and then you hear someone saying, 'These are real warriors!' No, they're not! They're not fucking warriors! Warriors put on Kevlar vests and load M4s, and*

when they go to work somebody dies and somebody lives. There's nothing about it that's a sport or fun or good at all". (Interview by Clay Skipper & Nick Marino, photo by Martin Schoeller)

Living in a time of peace does not excuse anyone from training and neither does age. As we get older, it is important to remember that the more active the body remains the healthier it will be. I am constantly bombarded with people who come to me and say, "I would love to train in the martial arts, or lift weights or work out in general, but I'm just too old." As always, I do my best to remain polite and acknowledge their thoughts to a point, but I always counter with this, "If you had a loved one that was being attacked, would you help?" Or would you stand back and let the attack occur because you're too old? All will answer, "I will help!" My response then is, "Why not prepare now?"

Having martial discipline and always being "on guard" can be a difficult thing to do but once you start to actively train the mind, you begin to look for things that most people ignore, find exits points while others remain focused on their cell phones or what's immediately in front of them and study the habits and behaviors of those around you. It's like an atrophied muscle that starts to get used again, your mind starts to become aware and alert, your instincts become sharper and you're better prepared to deal with danger before it occurs, in some cases you may even be able to remove yourself from the situation.

Be ready, be focused, Stand Fast!

Study strategy over the years and achieve the spirit of the warrior. Today is victory over yourself of yesterday; tomorrow is your victory over lesser men.

Miyamoto Musashi 宮本 武蔵

Samurai / Master Swordsman

AWAKENING THE WARRIOR MIND

Awakening

It's important to know that unless you are a psychopath/sociopath, most people do not want to fight and will generally do whatever they can to avoid it. The way you think and the way you respond has a lot to do with how you will react when a situation develops that requires you to become physical.

Once you understand that the "flight or fight" response is a real thing and that the fear that you are having is actually part of your mind's way of ensuring survival, you can then move forward and do what needs to be done, push fear off to the side and engage your opponent.

Training your mind will develop your instincts and, in some cases, warn you of danger before it occurs. Is this possible? Yes, in a way. Through your senses, the subconscious mind takes in a great amount of information, more information than the conscious mind can clearly process. As the mind absorbs the details of the information received, it may translate it into something that you can comprehend, that "something" can be interpreted as a feeling. The translated bit of information received will be that something is "wrong" or out of place with the person, people or with your immediate environment. This feeling is sometimes referred to as a gut feeling", hunch or woman's intuition.

Homicide detectives take as many pictures as they can of the crime scene so that they can continuously review them at a later time. When they get that "feeling" that something is not right, it is more likely that their subconscious mind has observed something that does not quite "fit", it might be days later when it finally hits them, but through dedicated observation something suddenly becomes obvious and they see what they've been missing.

Moral of the story? Trust your feelings...trust your instincts! Your subconscious mind has seen something that the conscious mind has been unable to process, open your eyes and become more aware of your surroundings. Train your mind in this way, and your instincts will become stronger, your powers of observation will increase. An author by the name of Gavin DeBecker wrote a book titled *The Gift of Fear*. In this book he talks to some victims and asks the question, what did you "feel" right before the incident? Almost all said that they felt that something was wrong with the situation but also felt that they were imagining  it and didn't want to judge or offend the person they were dealing with, causing them to disregard their instincts. One particular case was that of a young lady entering into her apartment building, one of those with a security entranceway. She had groceries in her hands and was in the process of negotiating how she was going to juggle the groceries and manipulate the keys to open the door when she was approached by a well-dressed young man who volunteered to assist her. She admitted afterwards that she felt uneasy about him and didn't feel comfortable with his approach but ignored those feelings, he was, after all, well dressed and looked like a nice guy. That person held the victim captive for several days, repeatedly raping and abusing her.

Trust your instincts!!! Like any muscle, left unused, your natural survival instincts will become atrophied and weak, the more you become aware and listen to those "feelings", the stronger they will become. Have a talk with any combat veteran about this subject, at the end of that conversation you may not ever question the need to trust and develop your instincts.

From my own experience, I learned to trust my instincts and rely on them during any operation. There were plenty of times when my target, and by that, I mean the person I had targeted for the operation, was trying to lure me into an area other than the agreed upon destination. A place convenient for them but would leave me, or a member of our team, with no backup, an advantage for them and bad for us. Number one rule was, besides safety, never be afraid to walk away from a "deal". I remember vividly when my instincts would tell me to walk away, when my level of danger had gone beyond my ability to properly defend myself. I walked away every single time, well, except for once, and that one could have gone extremely bad if I had let it get further. On that day, my ego had taken charge and the target that I had was a high priority, I wanted to make sure that I would be the one responsible for his arrest. I compromised my personal safety that day and let my ego take me further than I should have. I could have been hurt, or worse, had I not stopped myself and realized that I was going in over my head and that my target could be arrested at a later time without compromising my safety or that of our team. I walked away, something that was incredibly hard to do, we made arrangements and did the deal at a later time, he was arrested then.

Any type of combatives or martial arts training should start first by developing the warrior mind. You can train the physical body to peak performance, you can have an awesome beach body and impress the opposite sex, but a weak mind and/or a poor mental attitude will not make you a better fighter. Let's not kid ourselves, that is exactly what we are talking about here, you are not training and developing yourself to be a "Ken" doll, you are developing the warrior, and that starts with the mind. Focusing on your appearance first is like a beautiful sword that is forged from cheap metal, it is nice to display but has no real purpose or use. Is that your intent? My students often hear me say that I would rather have a student with "heart" but no skill then skill and no "heart". Skill, with time and effort, can be taught, but having no "heart", that's worthless. That's the minimalist, the one that does just enough to get by.

Focus first on developing your mind and mental attitude. You are like that sword that I mentioned, currently in the process of being forged. We all have seen this process and have a good visualization of what it looks like. The forge is your gym, the blacksmith is your coach and you are the sword. The constant pounding, folding and beating of the metal is your training, the more you repeat this process, the stronger you will become. You were not made to be a sword on display, you were designed and forged for battle and the only way that the blade can be ready is to push yourself and survive the process. We will discuss this further in greater detail, and by that, I mean I'm gonna get really deep into the whole sword metaphor.

> *"We all have self-doubt. You don't deny it, but you also don't capitulate to it. You embrace it."-Kobe Bryant*

KNIGHTS OATH

*Be without fear in the
face of your enemies.*

*Be brave and upright,
that God may love thee.*

*Speak the truth always,
even if it leads to your death.*

Safeguard the helpless and do no wrong;

RISE A KNIGHT.

Kingdom of Heaven
2005 Movie directed by Ridley Scott

HOKA HEY (It is a good time to Die)

Hoka Hey was the Lokota war cry used by the great war chief Crazy Horse used as a reminder that at that particular time, at that moment, you may die, but dying in defense of your people and traditions is a good way to die. Being afraid to die changes nothing, you'll die anyway, being afraid will only affect the way you live. Living the most you can before those final moments is why it is so important to think about death.

Every warrior culture in one form or another should always keep in mind that they are finite beings and death awaits us all, there is no escaping nature's number one rule, yeah, it's not taxes, some people don't pay taxes. At any time, life can be taken from you and whatever you're planning or currently doing will abruptly come to an end, it's not meant to be morbid, it's simply a reminder.

The Samurai always kept death in the forefront of everything they did, when the first Europeans encountered this culture, some made the misconception that they worshipped death because of their never-ending contemplation of it. As a warrior culture, it really had less to do with death and everything to do with acceptance. How you died was directly related to your life, honor and legacy. Musashi, Samurai and philosopher wrote *"Generally speaking, the Way of the warrior is a resolute acceptance of death"*. A warrior that has accepted the possibility that death can happen at any time is prepared and ready for it, this makes for a prepared and dangerous adversary.

The term "Momento Mori", a Latin phrase originating in ancient Rome meaning " remember that you must die", became popular in medieval European culture. Many adorned themselves with objects like skulls or dying flowers to symbolize mortality. Living in a time where death was common, it was a reminder that every day was important and death could be found anywhere. Marcus Aurelius, Roman Emperor and philosopher, wrote *"You could leave life right now. Let that determine what you do and say and think."* Again, as many past and future warriors would learn, he wasn't focused on death, he was focused on remembering that death was inevitable part of life, therefore life must be lived to the fullest.

Thinking of death does not make you morbid or depressing, it makes you appreciate what you have and the precious gift that life is. The Guazabara Federation logo has a small skull on the lower corner as a reminder, not of death, but of life. It is a additionally a constant reminder of the one thing that we all have in common and the reality of what you are learning.

 *"It is good to have a reminder of death before us, for it helps us to understand the impermanence of life on this earth, and this understanding may aid us in preparing for our own death. He who is well prepared is he who knows that he is nothing compared with Wakan-Tanka who is everything; then he knows that world which is real."* -Black Elk, Lakota Spiritual Adviser

ENERGY

When you're in a field that trains combatives and police tactics, the topic of energy, the Chinese Chi, Japanese/Korean ki or the Polynesian Mana is something that is seldom brought up. Unless you study the internal martial arts, most martial systems don't talk about what energy is or how it can be gathered.

Before I go any further, I would like you to think of different ways that you've felt energy but were probably not even aware that it was happening. Ever gone into a child's nursery and felt the power there? It's a feeling of wellbeing and comfort. If you're upset or angry, it's amazing how fast your mood changes. It's the reason holy places and sacred lands have so much strong mana, all the prayers and positive thinking causes a continuous echo of energy to seep into everything there, that coupled with the natural energy that is already there makes it special. Know an example of negative energy? Crime scene specialists will tell you that after years of police work and being at so many crime scenes, you begin to "feel" negative energy, it washes over you like extreme sorrow or depression. Once you recognize that subtle feeling, you begin to feel it in other places as well, even places that you have never previously visited. You understand that something bad has happened there, terrible enough to have left an imprint.

Energy permeates your body and all living objects. There are people that always seem to radiate one form or another. Some will make you feel good or bad the minute they arrive, you know this, everyone has felt this at one time or another. Those people that are always negative and seem to be surrounded in a cloud of depression will affect your mood if you are not guarded and aware, limit your contact with them, most often you can't change their way of thinking anyway. On the other side of that, you will meet those that when they arrive anywhere, you immediately feel good just being in their presence, they're the type of people that you will often hear others say when they arrive, now the party has started.

You are 100% in control of how others perceive you and the energy that surrounds you. In the Korean methods of understanding energy and human behavior, there is a practice called Nunchi, (눈치). It's your ability to measure a person's mood and energy upon first contact. We all have this ability, it's especially prevalent when it's someone you already know. You might ask, "Are you alright?" Most won't even know that you have picked up on the subtle change in their behavior until you bring it up, they may not even be aware that the energy surrounding them has changed. I train a great deal of people in physical combatives, tactics and warrior mindset. Those that are training as part of a mandatory training program are the ones that I use to practice my nunchi skills the most. Some are excited to learn something new and will even ask questions and perform the drills continuously until they begin to get a rudimentary understanding of what is being taught. Then there are those that enter the training area full of negative energy with no desire to learn, with these I am reminded that it's easier to teach a cat to fetch then to train someone with a closed mind.

You can gather into yourself both negative and positive energy and the energy you gather can be used to motivate you or bring you down and make you depressed. Surround yourself with positive thinking people and you will feel the same way, in some cases their attitude might even be a direct reflection of you.

While studying Hapkido in South Korea, I was amazed at how much emphasis was placed on moving and gathering energy. In Hapkido, the practice of Dahn Jon Ho Hup is similar to Tai Chi or Qi Gong, in that it's designed to gather energy inside you in preparation for conflict, confrontation or stressful events. The masters of this, in my opinion, are the Maori people, who with their Haka, challenge and intimidate their opponent while drawing mana into themselves in preparation for battle, to simply see this is to see and feel their power.

"If you want to find the secrets of the universe, think in terms of energy, frequency and vibration." Nikola Tesla

CODE OF CONDUCT

In most cultures, a Warrior is most often a fighter, but a fighter is not necessarily a Warrior. Why is that? As I have stated before, there are three components that must be filled before one can lay claim to the title of warrior. Defense of those in need, service to others and living by a morale code of conduct. A warrior will follow a certain set of guidelines, a code of conduct if you will, they adhere to this code and live their lives by it. Holding themselves to this strict set of rules, rules that they will not break, helps keep them on their chosen path.

It can vary from person to person, it may even be extremely private. It's my opinion, that's what separates a warrior from the thug is the Code. This code generally has to do with personal honor and integrity. You take a look at history and you will see the many ancient warrior societies such as the medieval knights of Europe or the Japanese

Bushi (Samurai) Class all had a Rule of Conduct, regulating their behavior. But here is the "kicker", just because you have rules, and you swear that you will never break those rules, doesn't mean that you won't. The human factor always plays a role, and for many, history has proven that those rules were often broken or corrupted.

During times of major crises and personal pain, the rules often get difficult to follow and can be broken, but not without damage. Many who leave the path or stray far from their original guidelines find it difficult to live with this violation and will most often look for redemption by returning to their original core values. Others might attempt to justify their actions and "adjust" their code to fit what they have done; this generally leads down a dark path.

When I refer to the "way" I'm speaking of living the Warrior Way of life. It's more than fighting, it's a lifestyle of discipline, honor and integrity. The follower of the "way" understands that their chosen path of life is difficult but will often lead to success. You want to live in the "way"? Start first by developing your own personal code.

"Waste no more time arguing what a good man should be. Be one." -Marcus Aurelius
Roman Emperor and Philosopher

**The Seven Virtues of Bushido -
The Way of the Warrior**
義 **Gi-Justice**

禮 **Rei-Respect**

勇 **Yu-Courage**

名誉 **Meiyo-Honor**

仁 **Jin-Compassion/ Benevolence / Mercy**

誠 **Makoto-Honesty**

忠義 **Chu-Loyalty**

BE THE ALPHA

When I first designed the Combatives training for the local Sheriff's department, I knew what needed to be done but the quandary that I quickly found myself in was that not everyone was able to perform at the level that was expected. If I lowered the standard, it's a disservice to those that perform at higher levels.

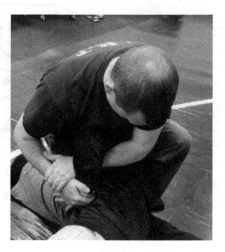

I believed that it would take a great amount of training for them to achieve the level that was necessary for them to utilize those skills in a time of crises, unfortunately there were others who, either did not have the athletic ability or simply had no desire to train. The Sheriff had made the decision that the training was absolutely necessary, all members from the three divisions, Public Safety, Corrections, and Court Security would need to complete the course.

With this information, I began to design a program that everyone would be able to perform. Utilizing the type of format that the military had been doing for years, I put together a basic combatives training curriculum (White Belt) that would apply for everyone and then added what I termed as Alpha training (Blue Belt) for those that wanted to go further.

Alpha training is usually what I refer to as a higher level of training given to those that, not only want to train, but because of the nature of their specific jobs, require their training to be more advanced.

What do I mean by Alpha? For me, the Alpha is a unique being, willing to try new things and challenge themselves. They are also your "go getters", those that are willing to do the hard work and step up when things are destined to get difficult. They complain less, work more, push themselves harder and expect more. These are your military special forces, CRT (Correction Response Team), SWAT (Special Weapons & Tactics), special units and all those that go above and beyond their expected duties, hopefully this is you. Alphas don't hesitate to get that extra level of training and are always willing to help others move to their higher levels. They have fallen and failed more times than they can count, they know what defeat tastes like because it's a familiar flavor but they always get back up, they don't believe in losing, they never lose....they either win or they learn.

What about all the others? They are often afraid to fail, so they never try, they are the ones who want what the Alpha has, but don't want the work associated with it. Their thoughts are often focused on personal benefits and not on how their actions may affect the team or the mission, they fail to see the big picture. When a problem is presented to an Alpha, they focus on the solution, when that same problem falls in the lap of the others, they look at who caused the problem, who's to blame and why isn't someone else fixing it.

So, this brings me back to training. It is important that everyone is

trained equally. All your basic levels and fundamentals are designed with everyone in mind, from your highest denominator to the lowest, all must be trained. When we train and coach, we understand that this is not for competition, for trophies or awards, we do so with the knowledge that the skills that we learn or pass on may save a life, a heavy responsibility.

Alpha training is the highest level of training. These are the skills taught to those who are willing to accept, with an ego free attitude, the knowledge that is being passed to them. Whether it's martial arts, defensive tactics or advanced firearms training, the trainer knows that these higher levels are difficult to teach and even more difficult to learn. For the trainee to acquire muscle memory and skill they must first have the patience to do multiple repetitions and drills.

Never forget who and what you are! When you falter and second guess your abilities, always keep in mind that you are already doing something that others won't.

"Out of every one hundred men, ten shouldn't even be there, eighty are just targets, nine are the real fighters, and we are lucky to have them, for they make the battle. Ah, but the one, one is a warrior, and he will bring the others back."

Heraclitu (Ἡράκλειτος, *Herakleitos)* 535 BC -475BC.

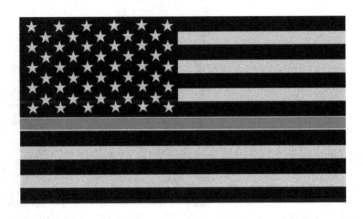

We have an incredible warrior class in this country - people in law enforcement, intelligence - and I thank God every night we have them standing fast to protect us from the tremendous amount of evil that exists in the world. -Brad Thor, Author

THE MANY MINDS OF THE WARRIOR

The Japanese Warrior/Bushi class was known as the Samurai. These warriors believed that the human mind varied depending on what the individual was currently involved with or doing, the many minds of the warrior was the warrior's state of mind during these specific times.

Shoshin (Empty Cup)

The Beginner's Mind. The empty cup willing and ready to be filled with knowledge. Most student's when they first enter the dojo or training hall come in with this mind. They are open and ready to absorb new information regardless of personal experience, allowing them to accept new ideas and concepts. This open mindset is very important for the student that is continuously learning and growing. The shoshin mind needs to be fed with knowledge and skill and the teacher is only too happy to do just that.

Zanshin (Stand Fast)

The hyperfocused mind, totally present and in the moment, 100% aware of his surroundings. This is the mind prepared and ready to spring into action. The Zanshin mind is the person who is the ready mind, ready to move, to attack or to act. In the military and police, as mentioned earlier, this state of being is often described using the term,

"Stand Fast", it means stand ready. The Zanshin mind is focused and ready to respond to any situation. It's a heightened sense of vigilance. Utilizing Cooper's color code of readiness, this subject is in a state of orange readiness (We'll talk more about this later).

Mushin

Also known as Mushin No-shin. This is a state of Empty Mind. Not to be confused with being mindless. Empty Mind is a mental state of being in the moment, a place of total mindfulness, the Zen mind. Through continuous training and the application of certain movements, a martial arts student may enter into a state of Mushin, 100% focused on what they are doing and not cluttered by outside events, issues and/or emotions. By continuous repetition of movement, the practitioner falls into this state of being, a moving meditation where there is nothing in existence other than you and your training.

Fudoshin

The Committed Mind. I mind with a single purpose, focused and unbending. In times of immense adversity, the Fudoshin mind will remain stead fast and will refuse to waiver. Athletes, entrepreneurs and warriors of all types will put themselves in a state of Fudoshin to accomplish their goals.

"Don't focus on what you think you deserve. Take aim at what you are willing to earn."

-David Goggins
Navy SEAL (ret.)
Army Ranger School Graduate
U.S. Air Force TACP
Author of *You Can't Hurt Me*.

Isshin

The Ultimate Focused Mind. A state of mind that every specialist or martial artist strives for as they are performing a task that requires pinpoint focus. Those that are in a state of Isshin will not allow outside forces to distract them, they are the master of themselves. The sniper as he prepares to perform his duties is in a state of pure Isshin.

"A good shot must necessarily be a good man since the essence of good marksmanship is self-control and self-control is the essential quality of a good man."

Theodore Roosevelt

NOTE: *Just as a point of total understanding, it is important to know that there are more "minds" than the ones that were discussed here. I chose these because it was my belief that they are the ones that you will feel and encounter the most both in your regular activities, tactical training and martial arts. If you have the desire, I encourage you to research this more.*

RULES OF ENGAGEMENT

According to the Encyclopedia Britannica, the Rules of Engagement are generally considered a military term that describes the way  combat between two forces is conducted. It is a recognition that has the opponents follow a set of procedures and standards that dictate their actions in a combative situation.

In this respect, the Code of Conduct that we spoke about earlier is different than the Rules of Engagement. Rules are defined by a set of standards and guidelines often dictated by honor and personal beliefs.

But you must always assume that the enemy that you have encountered follows no rules governing their actions, they are free to do as they will. This may put you in a state of quandary as it can become difficult to win in battle while fighting an opponent whose battle tactics are not governed or controlled.

There is no simple way, the easy path is often walked by cowards and fools. Push yourself to a higher level, train to be better than your opponent and always assume your opponent is better than you.

When teaching Police Combatives, this issue is constantly addressed. Learning to control a suspect while they are fighting is very difficult.

They are allowed to do to you what you cannot do to them. In this respect I remind those that are training, that the martial arts are much easier than police combatives. In the martial arts, two opponents can face each other in the streets and meet on equal terms but in a police conflict there are no equal terms. The officer can only seek to control a person who wishes them harm and follows no rules. Ever try controlling someone who is actively trying to fight you? Try it sometime, you may get a new understanding on what police officers deal with every day.

Can the Rules of Engagement change? Yes, to a point. A situation that involves deadly force will raise your response to a higher level, thus altering the Rule to complete the mission. But make no mistake, once you have completed what needs to be done, then you must return to the original "setting" or risk becoming that which you have trained to oppose.

Knowing how to fight but being governed by a set of guidelines is the most difficult part of all but that's the warrior way, nothing is easy.

With this understanding you train. You train to defend as well as to control, to diffuse and defeat. The role of defender and protector is what defines the warrior and separates them from the fighter. The warrior stands ready to defend those in need and master their emotions in such a way that their opponent cannot use it against them.

Whether on attack is physical-assault, rape, murder or whether it is mental-business intrigues, emotional abuse-you must be prepared for conflict by learning as much self-defense as possible, you will not become a bully or a monster, but instead you will learn that you can respond to any situation. If you are never attacked, that will be wonderful. Training will still help you work out your fears, inhibitions and anxieties.

365 Tao, Daily Meditations

by

Deng Ming Dao

WARRIORS FALL (But They Never Quit!)

FAILURE IS 100% ACCEPTABLE! When we came to the end of 2020, we all became acutely aware of how much we were all influenced by outside events that we had little or no control over. In 2020, the COVID-19 epidemic and politics were the obvious big ones. How much did those events affect the personal promises we made to ourselves? Did we fail to accomplish some of those goals  that we told ourselves that we would do before this year came to a close? I know I did, and I bet you did too. We are all flawed human beings; we want more for ourselves and struggle to keep up with all those things that it takes to accomplish all of them. Make yourself one small promise that you know you will be able to keep, from that you will build up to the next step and the next. Before you know it, you will have created a personal formula for success. Those small wins are very important, think of them as battle skirmishes that will lead you to victory.

Failure is 100% acceptable! Why do I say this? First and foremost, it means that you have goals to begin with and that you're willing to push yourself beyond where you were yesterday. What is unacceptable? Failing to get up after you fall! The defeat comes when you fail to continue. History is full of leaders and heroes who failed over and over but, because of personal discipline and a "never give up" attitude, continued to persevere and eventually were victorious. One such hero that comes to mind as I share this story with you is Audie L. Murphy, a hero of World War II. After the attack on Pearl Harbor, Murphy falsified his identification and attempted to enter the Armed Forces. Turned down initially for being too small and underweight by the Army, Marines and Navy (yes, he tried to get into all three branches). He continued his efforts until he was eventually able to enlist in the Army. He first saw combat in 1943 in the allied invasion of Sicily, then in 1944 The battle of Anzio, the liberation of Rome and the invasion of Southern France. Murphy fought at Montélimar and successfully led his men in battle into eastern France. He ended up being one of the most decorated combat soldiers of World War II. Imagine if he would have chosen to give up immediately after being denied entry into the Armed Services? How about if he had given up after each battle? He was so small that when he originally arrived in his unit, an annoyed supervisor assigned a soldier to keep an eye on him so that he would not be hurt, that soldier quickly learned that Murphy did not become a soldier to observe and found himself unable to keep up with him.

Murphy is a great example of a warrior who didn't start out as a fighter but through perseverance and indomitable will, became the man he was meant to be.

When you have goals and start fighting to achieve them, you will find roadblocks that will slow your progress and even stall you for long periods of time, so what, get over yourself! Be mindful that although you may be a flawed being, we all are, you will not give up. You may move slowly but you do that by heading in a forward direction, always advancing.

"If you're not failing, you're not trying.
You're living in some comfort zone.
You're not expanding."
-David Meltzer

"I don't know what bravery is, sometimes it takes more courage to get up and run than to stay.

You either do it or you don't. I got so scared the first day in combat I just decided to go along with it."

"Loyalty to your comrades, when you come right down to it, has more to do with bravery in battle than even patriotism does. You may want to be brave, but your spirit can desert you when things really get tough.

Only you find you can't let your comrades down and in the pinch, they can't let you down either."

Audie Murphy, Soldier

U.S Army

World War II

YOU'RE NOT A CAN OF SOUP

If I took a can of soup off the shelf and ripped off the label, how would you be able to tell what's in it? Think about this for a second. Without actually opening the can, what would you do to determine its contents.

There is no way, you have to open the can and find out...it's the only way. People will often judge you by your appearance, by what you do for a living or the clothes that you wear and yes, even for the  color of your skin. This is just basic human nature, even if you are consciously trying not to think that way, some of those negative thoughts will still creep into your head. Okay, so you've been judged, so what? You're not a can of soup, the label placed on you does not determine the contents, no one but you really know what's inside...only you know that. If you can agree with me on this point then why would you allow others to determine your worth, to tell you that you're a can of soup and nothing more.

People will often live by the labels that are placed on them and spend their time paying attention to the opinions of others. With the advent of social media, this has now been amplified. Young people who have not had the opportunity to build strong personal guards against such talk are inundated with a large amount of traffic via the internet. They're told what looks good and bad and constantly fed a large dosage of information on what others have determined perfection is, leaving many feeling inferior and inadequate.

Society has now entered a new phase, social censorship. People have now become unwilling to take ownership and make themselves stronger, instead they depend on others to shield them from everything bad. The fact is that we live in a free society and part of that is the acceptance of free speech, whether you agree with it or not, it will often place you in a position with people who will say and do things that you will not necessarily agree with, it's called life, we have to become strong enough to accept the good and the bad.

 What's inside you is who you truly are, you have the power to become strong, not just physically (which is easy in comparison) but mentally and spiritually. People will say and do things to you that may cause you great harm and unless you learn to develop some type of mental fortitude and shield yourself from them, you will always be their victim.

While I agree that people who use negative words are bullies, and I hate bullies, my job has always placed me in the position to teach others how to defend themselves from that type of behavior. We will never rid the world of bullies, listen to what I just said...never! It's a Yin Yang thing, there is balance in knowing that with every good person that you meet, there will always be an asshole out there as well, it's only a matter of time until you deal with them.

You're not a can of soup, if you're wearing a label that someone else has placed on you, rip it off! You have the ability to reinvent yourself, do it, never give others the power to determine your worth! Be who you were meant to be, don't let others determine who they think you should be or who you are. Bruce Lee had many words of wisdom that he would share, one that is less popular than most but a favorite of mine is, *"Always be yourself, have faith in yourself, do not go out and look for a successful personality and duplicate it"*.

Always treat others with respect and dignity but never deny yourself the same. Being good to yourself starts by not listening and accepting the negative opinions of others. What others think of you matters little, what you think of yourself matters greatly.

"If you have no critics, you'll likely have no success".

-Malcolm X

From Slave to Samurai

In 1579, when a group of Portuguese Jesuit missionaries arrived in Japan, they brought with them a slave whose real name has been lost but is remembered by the name given to him by the Japanese, Yusuke.

During this time, few African slaves had been seen by the Japanese, so it is said that when the Daimyo, Nobunaga, first saw Yasuke, he did not believe that his skin was black and made him take off his shirt to confirm that it was not paint or ink. When he found out that it was not, he was curious and incredibly interested in him and wanted to learn more about him.

Yasuke and the Jesuits continued their tour of Japan and met several other prominent figures. After returning to the court of Nobunaga, it is said that the Daimyo was so impressed with Yusuke's strength & prowess that he was taken into his service.

Shortly after that, and several battles later, Yasuke became the 1st Black Samurai.

THE THREE FACES

The Japanese say you have three faces.

The first face,

you show to the World.

The second face,

you show to your close friends and your family.

The third face,

you never show anyone.

It is the truest reflection of who you are.

THE SHARPENING STONE

As I mentioned in the last topic, I dislike the bully and everything that goes with it. In all my years of police work, I came across three types, I'm sure there are more but I'm not a specialist, I can only share with you my experience. The first is the one that we're most familiar with is the physical bully, they prey on those that are weak and unable to defend  themselves, they're intellectually inferior and attack others for the simple satisfaction of feeling superior. The second is the even bigger coward, the internet bully, the trolls, they don't even have the decency to look their victims in the face, their tool of the trade is the technology and they use it as a weapon and attack via texting, social media and emails. They say and do terrible things, hoping to elicit a response from the person they have chosen to torment. The last is the most devious, this is the one that pretends to be a friend but slowly and methodically sabotages anything their victim does, they will often say things to their "friend" like, "Quit trying to do this, you're not good enough, fast enough or smart enough." These are your classic "Crabs in a barrel", they want to keep their intended target from rising to a higher level and leaving them behind. The true friend encourages, promotes and pushes, wanting you to rise above the clouds and sore like eagle.

 Now, although we hate bullies, it is important to understand that adversity can be looked on as an ally rather than an enemy if you are able to recognize it for what it is. It's similar to training on the mat, if your opponent is better than you, it can be frustrating and demoralizing, but if you don't let it stop you, you may find your skills improving a little every day. This will not occur if your opponent is either your equal or not at your level. That's why many who train in the martial arts often looking for a skilled Uke (training partner) so that they can improve. In the beginning of your training, you should not attempt to best your opponent, simply try to delay their victory by surviving as long as you can. As your skills begin to improve you may notice that your opponent need's to work harder in order to defeat you. Moving forward, as the training continues, you will start improving to the level that you start winning the encounters.

As I said in the beginning of this book, the Dojo can be a symbol of life, in this case you can see the similarities. We improve and reach those higher levels with the help of others, in the training hall we have our training partners, our Uke's, in life we have adversaries, enemies, and bullies. They are our Sharpening Stones, we don't like them yet we need them, they make us stronger, we use them to "grind our blade" while they slowly wear down.

When I entered the U.S. Air Force, a very long time ago, I suffered from low self-esteem. I remember thinking that there was just nothing very special about me. There was one individual, a real douchebag, that joined the Air Force with the same bully like mentality that he had in high school. He enjoyed reminding me how much better than me  he was and that no matter what I did, he would always be better and do better. But the thing about the military is, those that join, come in all sizes and colors and from a wide variety of backgrounds, no one really seemed to care what you were or where you came from, as long as you could do what needed to be done and could back it up. I measured myself against this idiot and at every point I beat him. Looking back, I wasn't stronger, faster or even better than my nemesis, I just wanted it more. I remember one of the last events before basic graduation was the obstacle course, my "friend" said to me, "You'll be lucky if you even finish the course". Toward the end I remember crawling over a rope net, looking down at the nasty swamp below and seeing my "buddy" swimming his way to the edge, he had raced so fast to get ahead of me that he lost his balance and fell in. On graduation day, he left telling me that no matter what I did, he would always be better than me, I remember saying to him "Keep telling yourself that, maybe someday you'll even believe it. I wasn't even

 being angry. I was satisfied that I had been able to accomplish things that surprised even me. It was now time to move on to my new assignment and I felt better in mind and body because of my enemy, I made myself better and although I didn't know it at the time, that would be my first experience turning someone into my personal sharpening stone.

In the end, challenge and adversity can be a powerful ally if you have strength to see it and use it as that.

The similarities between the forging of a blade and a human being are unmistakable. To be strong and resilient you will need to push yourself beyond your self-imposed limitations.

"Iron is full of impurities that weaken it; through forging it becomes steel and is transformed into a razor-sharp sword."

Morihei Ueshiba

The Art of Peace

Founder of the Japanese Martial Art of Aikido

Student of Takeda Sokaku (Aiki-Jujitsu)

The Making of a Japanese Sword

"First, the pieces of raw steel were heated in the furnace to about 1,300 °C, resulting in a basic block of steel. After impurities were removed, the steel was repeatedly heated and beaten, then continuously folded back upon itself so as to create a complex structure with several layers. The steel for the outer skin received the most folding.

Next, the two separate pieces were combined. Whatever method was used, the outer skin would enclose the core of the sword along its length until just short of the tip. With heating and hammering, the combined steels were slowly drawn into the rough but recognizable outline of a Japanese blade". -The Samurai: The Making of a Japanese Sword by Stephen Turnbull

The War on Integrity

The dictionary describes Integrity as "the quality of being honest and having strong moral principles; moral uprightness". It would seem that in today's society the idea of having integrity has become a foreign old-fashioned concept. Our leaders and political figures  sacrifice their honor for status and money and betray their promises to satisfy personal gain. Is this a modern phenomenon or has it always been the case? As a matter of historical fact, the past has shown us that most leaders and people of power have abused their authority at the expense of those that they were sworn to represent or help.

It only feels like these times are worse simply because we are living them now and our access to the news and media is abundant, supplying us with more information than we have ever had. Today social media has increased to such a level that people in power find it extremely difficult to hide their acts of deceit.

We are bombarded by examples of those that cheat, steal and disrespect others yet are striving and succeeding in their chosen fields, some even make little to no attempt to hide this fact, and even capitalize on it. The rest of society conveniently ignores these actions while even more will begin to look up to those that seem to have a weak moral compass. They may see them as heroes and mentors because they envy their lifestyle, the flash, and money. The message is received, honor and integrity is malleable and not as rigid as they may have once been led to believe. To succeed and achieve the goal that they have set for themselves, their personal code of conduct needs to be sacrificed or at least "bent". In an effort to come to term with this, they tell themselves, "It's okay, when I reach my goal, I will get myself back on track."

It is my belief that taking something like integrity and honor and putting it on a shelf will tarnish the warrior's soul leaving wounds that can scar. It is incredibly difficult to come back from things like this, ask any survivor of an addiction. Many who have chosen to walk that path will cheat a little to accomplish their goals and then, when their goals have been reached, rather than attempting to retrieve their honor, they move the bar a little further away, making excuses as to why it is necessary and how the ends justify the means. As the author, Paulo Coelho says, *"There are no ends, there are only means".*

Walking into the darkness is something that every warrior has wrestled with at least once. I think life sends us these tests to see how we will react, they come to us in all sizes and methods. Guard your honor, protect your integrity, they are directly connected to your soul and your soul is the most precious gift that you've ever received.

The Warrior sense of honor should be paramount in your behavior, let others live by your example and use you as the guidepost for their way of living.

"Commanders must have integrity; without integrity, they have no power. If they have no power, they cannot bring out the best in their armies. Therefore, integrity is the hand of warriorship". -Sun Bin, Chinese General & Military Strategist

THE MAN IN THE ARENA

"Citizenship in a Republic"

"It is not the critic who counts; not the man who points out how the strong man stumbles, or where the doer of deeds could have done them better. The credit belongs to the man who is actually in the arena, whose face is marred by dust and sweat and blood; who strives valiantly; who errs, who comes short again and again, because there is no effort without error and shortcoming; but who does actually strive to do the deeds; who knows great enthusiasms, the great devotions; who spends himself in a worthy cause; who at the best knows in the end the triumph of high achievement, and who at the worst, if he fails, at least fails while daring greatly, so that his place shall never be with those cold and timid souls who neither know victory nor defeat."

Theodore Roosevelt

YOU GOT THE GIFT!

When we think of some of our greatest athletes and watch them doing what they do best, we often think, "Damn, they got the gift, I wish I was born with a gift like that! But the truth of the matter is that some talent is indeed natural but to develop the skill needed to achieve a high level of greatness requires a lot more than natural talent. It requires hard work, discipline and iron focus. Athletes like Kobe Bryant, Muhamed Ali, Billie Jean King and Roberto Clemente graced us with their presence, they were a true joy to watch and loved by many. But for every one of them, there are thousands, truly thousands who were born with skill but lacked the other ingredients necessary to rise above the rest. They are the unheard-of athletes who did not have the fortitude to push themselves further.

Those blessed with skill need to understand that in many cases skill is not enough. It may open doors for you, but will they stay open? Things like personal drive, focus, motivation, and discipline are among some of the ingredients that the athletes mentioned above had. All of them were self-aware, they knew they had a gift, but to develop

skill hard work was required, they pushed themselves further and became the best at their craft.

How about those warriors that had it all and for some reason through no fault of their own, lost it? When the "gift" is taken away, only those that were able to go beyond their skillset survived and continued to excel, they passed the most painful of tests and continued to move forward. I think of all our heroic warriors in the military that have suffered terrible injuries and in spite of everything that has happened to them, they make themselves available to help others. In the wake of so much tragedy, many of them choose to focus on others and in doing so, helped themselves.

Again, being born with extraordinary gifts and talents is an amazing thing but talent alone seldom allows anyone to achieve their dreams. You want something? Don't depend just on your "gifts", fight for it!

Talent is God-given, be thankful.
Fame is man given, be humble.
Conceit is self-given, be careful.
-Guro Dan Inosanto,
Martial Arts Master & Teacher

WARRIOR TACTICS

The mind is your first defense in most dangerous situations, all the defensive tactics training in the world will do you absolutely no good if you have failed to prepare yourself mentally for high stress events like immediate danger, anxiety or injury. The Warrior, when faced with these types of scenarios will use similar tactics to what is used in fighting, they will focus on the current situation, find their balance and begin to look for avenues of survival. Situational Awareness is heightened while focusing on weapons (both theirs and the enemies), environment, terrain, location and possible escape routes.

Let's break them all down individually so that they can be properly understood.

1. Situational Awareness
2. Weapons
3. Environment
4. Terrain
5. Location
6. Escape Routes

1. **Situational Awareness** will help you properly forecast dangers  as they begin to develop. No matter how good of a fighter you are, if you're oblivious of your surroundings this can leave you vulnerable to unnecessary threats. Keep your eyes and ears open, do not allow yourself to get so hyperfocused that you fail to see an obvious threat. Tunnel Vision comes from fixating on one point so strongly that you fail to see all the dangers present in the immediate combat zone.

   NOTES:_____

   _____

2. **Weapons**. Is there a potential for a weapon to be used? Does my opponent have a weapon? What weapon is being used and what is my possible response. What are my weapons? What happens can be made available?

   NOTES:_____

   _____

3. **Environment.** Environment has a lot more to do than just the weather, it's about location, customs and pressure. It's the pressure that can turn a peaceful gathering into a violent mob. Not understanding the customs can make the most innocent of acts look offensive. Studying the environment of your current location will help you increase your potential for survival.

   NOTES:_____

   _____

4. **Terrain.** Where is the fight taking place? Are you standing on mud, concrete, rocks? Is the ground level or are standing on a slope? How will that impact the type of defense you were planning. Can you find a way to make it work in your favor?
   NOTES:_____

   _____

5. **Location.** Are you in a crowded place? Are there obstacles in your way? Are you in a foreign country and not familiar with your immediate surroundings? Prior to arriving in unfamiliar territory, research as much as you can, locate the nearest hospitals/clinics, police stations and places that can be considered safe zones in the cases of storms or catastrophes
   NOTES:_____

   _____

6. **Escape routes.** You can look at this from two different perspectives. Escape routes from a smaller perspective could mean something as simple as sitting down in a restaurant and locating all the exit points, if you don't see an obvious one, look for the kitchen, the exit is always there. From a larger point of view, you might be looking for roadways and highways that may help in evacuating you and your family during a catastrophe. Back roads seem like a good idea but they can get congested, washed out or flooded. These are good things to know. Obvious escape routes can sometimes be the most dangerous, if it's obvious to you, it's obvious to everyone else as well, avoid large groups, herds don't move well when panicked!

NOTES:_____

_____

NOTE: Use this as a reference. I left space for you to add your own personal notes and ideas. Think of places that you've already visited or are planning to visit. While you're planning that perfect vacation, look for negative possibilities as well, it's hard to think that way but it's always good to have a plan.

"The great majority of the victims of violent crimes are taken by surprise. The one who anticipates the action wins, the one who does not, loses. Learn from the experience of others and don't let yourself be surprised". - An excerpt from Principles of Personal Defense by Col. Jeff Cooper

COL. JEFF COOPER'S COLOR CODE OF AWARENESS.

70% of all defense is based on Awareness. Remain vigilant of your surroundings, see the danger before it occurs, have a plan and be ready to neutralize the threat.

White-State of complete unreadiness, oblivious to your surroundings. Unprepared and unready to take action.

Yellow-Prepared, alert and relaxed. Aware of your surroundings. Good situational awareness.

Orange-Specific problem noticed or a possible problem developing. Plan has been developed and you are ready to take action.

OBLIVIOUS
AWARE
ALERT
ENGAGED
FROZEN

Red-Action Mode. Completely focused on the emergency at hand. Awaiting mental trigger to launch response.

Black (Not originally one of Cooper's color code) Complete System Overload. Panic, breakdown of physical performance. Unable to function.

Col. John Dean "Jeff" Cooper (May 10, 1920 – September 25, 2006) was a U.S. Marine, combat pistol instructor and author who revolutionized handgun and rifle tactics by introducing such innovative methods of training that many of them are still in use as of today. He was the creator of the concept of the combat mindset and the Color Code of Awareness.

"I'VE GOT YOUR SIX?"

I've lost count of how many times I've had people tell me that they did not feel that there was any need to train, when the time comes for them to fight, they would be ready. *"Don't worry, I got your back"*. My answer to that is, and has always been, "No, you don't!" If Musashi's words are true, and *"We fight the way we train"*, then it stands to reason that lack of training equals lack of fighting. If you don't want to train, fine, that's on you, but don't lie to me or yourself, you are no one's back up and there's a good chance that your lack of training will get someone hurt.

There are those who understand that nothing good comes easy, but there are still a great many who would prefer the easier route. In today's day and age, many have become accustomed to being comfortable and getting rewarded for doing little. It's a part of our "fast food mentality" of instant gratification. But there are some things that cannot be rushed, some things that in order to be done correctly, have to be accomplished in the old ways, by simply training, repeating, sharpening and perfecting.

If you have chosen the warrior's path and accepted the responsibility that goes with it, then you need to understand that you will be the shield guarding those in need. Are you ready? If you are not properly prepared and trained, and you are depending on chance and luck, then you need to stop and reevaluate your chosen career path. You chose a warrior's path but you are NOT a warrior. Seems harsh? Think of all the reasons you chose this way of life, if you did it for status or money, please do everyone a favor and leave, just because you wear a warriors clothing does not make you one, those of us living the Way have seen plenty of these people, they're the reason police reputations have suffered so much.

I have been an instructor in the fighting arts for over forty years, training both police and civilians. During that time, I have trained many civilians who live the warrior lifestyle. Although their chosen careers are not that of a warrior, they nevertheless walk that path and train hard, not because they have to but because of who they are! If you are in a warrior's career such as first responder, military or security specialist then what right do you have not to train at the highest levels possible?

Make that hard decision to be the best version of yourself and then fight to get yourself there. There are no excuses!

No one wants to deal with conflict, but those who have, have always understood that it is best to be prepared. The person who says I'll be ready when the time comes is the same as the idiot who says, "I'll cross that bridge when I come to it." Not really sure who came up with that but I bet their lack of planning made them ill prepared for that bridge when they finally got there. Stupid thinking.

Imagine you are preparing for a marathon and the event takes place two months from today. If your plan is to complete this tremendous run then you will start preparing immediately. You will run a little more every day and make sure that you are taking the proper nutrients. You will want your body as strong as possible, knowing that a lack of planning is not an option. The difference is that your "marathon" could be tomorrow, next week, a month from now, or 10 years from now. You will never know when you will be tested. On the day that happens, please don't let your dying wish be, I should have trained harder.

"The martial way is not for everyone, fellow warrior. You are a special individual and that carries a heavy responsibility. Therefore, you must think, feel and act as a warrior in every situation. You represent a select cast, a noble profession. In the world of pomp and shabby facade, you must be tempered, polished and elite."

Living the Martial Way

by

Forest Morgan, Maj. USAF

THE WARRIORS CIRCLE

When we think of the Warrior Circle, it's with the knowledge and understanding that it is small. The Circle consists of those individuals that the Warrior surrounds themselves with, those that they associate with and can count on for support, advice, and most especially, understanding.

I cannot stress the importance of this group of allies, no one can do it alone and to think that you can is the highest level of arrogance. Show me the most successful people you know, the ones who can impact the most people and I'll show you their Warriors Circle. Even the late Martin Luther King, Jr. would not have been able to impact so many without his wife, Coretta Scott King, at his side, she was in his circle.

I often think of my time in South Korea, the close group of friends that I had and the level of friendship that we established. They were

my brothers, we did everything together, Dan, Rick, Scott (Taz), Chico and King. I think of them often and remember all the great memories, boys became men. They were members of my first circle, whether they knew it or not, they were all responsible for the path that I would someday walk. In time others would take their place, but none would have the impact as those first. They came into my life during a time when I was the most lost and alone. We were all kids, barely out of our teen's, and I learned something from each one of them. From Dan I learned about integrity, this dude would always do the right thing even if no one agreed with him. Rick taught me the meaning of honor, he was the ultimate Airmen, out of all of us, he was all in, I knew he would be in for life. Thirty years later I would attend his retirement and when the time came, he attended mine. Chico taught me how to have fun and squeeze the hell out of life, he was the only one of them that was not a cop, my Puerto Rican brother from another mother. I hope life was good to you bro, thanks for the mixed tape. King, he was like a little kid in the body of a giant. A big bear that was eternally in a good mood, don't remember if I ever saw him angry. Last was Scott, we were inseparable, we did a lot of good shit and really stupid shit together. We all called him Taz because he was like the Tasmanian Devil, he would never slow down, always on the move. Scott taught me the meaning of dedication. Always trying to help people and do the right thing. Later in life, Scott sacrificed his life saving others

while stationed at Hickam AFB, Hawaii. Thank you for always being there my friend, we will see each other again, first drinks on you.

Today, there are others in my circle and as always, it remains small.

Never make the mistake of thinking that you can do everything on your own, thinking that way has cost us too many good warriors. Choose them wisely, those in our circle have a great effect on our way of thinking and acting, they can push you forward or hold you back. We all need someone, sometimes just to keep us on point.

"Associate yourself with men of good quality if you esteem your own reputation; for 'tis better to be alone than in bad company".

-George Washington

American Founding Father

1st President of the United States

WHEN THE STUDENT IS READY THE TEACHER WILL COME

I'm sure at one point or another, everyone has heard the saying "When the student is ready, the teacher will come." I think I'm going to have to strongly disagree with this. This saying implies that the universe will take care of everything and you just have to sit back, relax, and wait for it to happen. It would be more accurate if it said, "When  the student is ready, the search can begin." That's what its gonna take...the will to accept, the need to improve and the desire to grow. Once all the ego has been set aside and the student is ready, then it's time to look for a qualified teacher that can help and guide you on your journey for self-improvement and discovery.

Surround yourself with people of good character and you will find yourself measuring up to their standard. There are teachers and mentors in the traditional sense but there are also many among our friends and acquaintances. Sometimes those same people don't have to say a word, just the way they live their lives is enough for you to look at them and mimic their positive behavior.

Back in the 80's, when the opportunity presented itself, I requested South Korea as my duty assignment. I had a mission, my martial arts instructor was there, I just needed to find him. Even before I received my orders, I knew I would be sent there and I would find a teacher.

 Upon my arrival in the country and properly settled in, I took a bus into town and started my search. My plan was to ask some of my fellow airmen if they knew of any martial art schools in the area. As amazing as it sounds, within an hour of walking around and exploring, I saw a poster in a store window advertising Hapkido. I entered the store and asked the shopkeeper if he knew the location of the instructor and the school. Between my broken Korean and his broken English, he was able to give me a rough idea of where the school was located. After finding the location described to me, I was disappointed to find out that it was not a Hapkido school but taught Tang Soo Do instead. I decided since I had come this far, I might as well check to see if the place was open and if someone there could help me out with my search. I entered and met the instructor, who greeted me warmly and, to my delight, spoke English very well. I explained to him what I was looking for and that a local shopkeeper had directed me to his Dojang. He was actually excited to help and let me know that the Hapkido teacher was a friend of his and taught Hapkido at his Dojang twice a week but his actual training facility was on the Air Force Base and

that he could be found there most days. He went on to say that he trained many Americans at his facility and that his school and the Hapkido school did a lot together. I learned that this was a common theme for smaller dojangs to work together when the styles were different but still complimented each other. I would later spend a great deal of time with him as he would help me prepare for a tournament in the Philippines. After receiving a business card for the Hapkido school, I left there and returned back to the base to continue my search.

I arrived at the base gym and was directed to the martial arts training area where I met my teacher, Master Yu Chong Su. We spent the next hour talking about Hapkido and the training I had received prior to arriving in Korea, he was interested in my background and the Hapkido lineage that I had. The next day, there I was, having dinner at his home thinking to myself that I had managed to find my martial arts teacher and was now having dinner with him less than twenty-four hours from arriving. I knew that the universe would help me but it wouldn't do all the work for me, I was given the puzzle but needed to put the pieces together.

Mentors, instructors and guides come in all forms, some stay with us for years and others for short moments. If you have an open mind and listen close you may learn something from each of them. I've had the privaledge of sharing drinks and sparring tips at a bar with a kickboxer  who apparently had a "Superfoot." I learned the importance of mixed martial arts while enjoying sushi with a Croatian MMA fighter from Iowa, spent the evening discussing music, ground combatives and Jiu-jitsu fundamentals from a Brazilian Champion who loved Bulldogs and received great advice from a Filipino Guro who once trained with a little dragon.

Ed Mylet, entrepreneur and philanthropist, has said that *"If you surround yourself with five people that are healthy and in shape, you will be the sixth, surround yourself with five people that are financially stable, you will again be the sixth."* I may not have quoted him perfectly, but you get the general idea, your people represent you.

We need our teachers and mentors; they help us bump up to the next level. Do not wait for them to come to you, open your heart and be ready to receive them while you're searching. Be wise about your mentors, it truly matters, search them out and be selective, they are very important to your growth and development and they can be found in the strangest places if you're willing to do your part.

"Be of Service to the thing you claim to Love."
-Russell Brand

KUZUSHI (崩し:くずし)

In many of the Japanese martial arts, most specifically Judo, there is a technique that is referred to as Kuzushi. Kuzushi is the art of breaking your opponent's balance, something that is very important before you perform a technique or a throw. Before you begin any technique, the  student first begins by disrupting the opponent's balance, this can be performed by either pushing or pulling the subject in such a manner that the technique they are planning can be more easily performed. Techniques performed without Kuzushi are much more difficult to perform because they were not designed to be done from a static position, understanding this allows you to properly comprehend the importance of removing your opponent's balance.

If Kuzushi is the act of physically disrupting the balance of your opponent, can this be done without contact? This in itself brings up an important issue that we as student warriors must learn to understand and deal with. Whether a battle is physical or psychological, when the fight occurs there is always one opponent attempting to disrupt the balance of the other. Do my words elicit a negative emotional response? Are you so angry at me because of something I did or said that all you want to do is attack? I have then effectively disrupted your balance; this action may allow me the upper hand. Understand this, if your mind continues to focus on negative past events and for some reason you are unable to come to terms with what you are feeling, this is the loss of balance. I am not an expert on the mind, I speak to you from a simple understanding of human nature and the art of the fight, and I am telling you the rules that apply in a physical confrontation will often mirror the psychological one.

If I have an enemy, and my enemy has a weak mind, my presence alone will be enough to take their balance. It is much easier to unbalance the mind then your body. Now if you are aware of this, guard your thoughts the way you would your body in a fight, make no mistake, it is a fight that you are in, the only difference is when you are dealing with your mind, you are your own opponent.

Years ago, I attended a martial arts event where my students would be demonstrating Guazabara Machete Fighting. It was one of the largest tournaments that I had ever been at. The martial arts host, a Korean TaeKwonDo master, had booked the entire hotel for the event. There was a problem with a few of the rooms and the TKD master quickly became frustrated with the employee on duty. The employee, to his credit, maintained a calm demeanor and tried to diffuse the situation. The master remained angry and disrespectful to him, stating that he believed he was not being treated with the respect that was due a person of his station. The hotel employee attempted to explain that he was not in a position to make any changes and that he would do the best he could to speak to the management and hopefully accommodate his guests. Instead of being satisfied with the employee's explanation, the master continued to raise his voice and lose his temper. As I watched, I remember thinking, this man has allowed such a trivial event to unbalance him, he is not in control of his thoughts or emotions. The hotel employee, who remained calm, maintained Kuzushi without even trying, he was balanced and in charge.

Learn to master your thoughts and to retain balance. Breath, relax and focus.

The happiness of your life depends upon the quality of your thoughts: therefore, guard accordingly, and take care that you entertain no notions unsuitable to virtue and reasonable nature. When you arise in the morning, think of what a precious privilege it is to be alive - to breathe, to think, to enjoy, to love. -Marcus Aurelius, Roman Emperor & Philosopher

THE POWER OF IMPACT

Martin Luther King, Jr. truly was a master of Impact, his ability to motivate those around him drove the Civil Rights movement and pushed many who were on the sidelines to step up and do their part. His "I Have A Dream" speech touched the human soul and is just as powerful today as it was back in 1963 when he shared it with the world.

When a person who trains others in the fighting arts and has spent a lifetime in the police field mentions the Power of Impact, others assume that what I'm talking about is striking, I am not. The Power of Impact I'm referring to is the ability to motivate and drive others to do and be the best versions of themselves. How else did a little nun from Calcutta, known throughout the world, become founder of an organization dedicated to serving the poor? Saint Mother Teresa's  ability to motivate people from all walks of life was directly connected to her power of love. The rich, poor, famous and unknown all felt it, it was not just what she said but how she made everyone feel, her overwhelming compassion for those in need reflected off of her like sunlight and her dedication to humanity was her gift to mankind. Her mere presence made everyone kinder, more compassionate and more loving, it wasn't so much what she said but how she lived. We are all better just by knowing that she existed, that, my dear friends, is Impact.

Mahatma Gandhi (Mohandas Karamchand Gandhi) was an Indian lawyer who, while living in South Africa, utilized non-violent methods to fight for Civil Rights. Later he would move back to India which was under British rule and organized the peasant farmers to  protest excessive tax and the inequality of the Indian people. Gandhi's anti-colonialism campaign started a sense of nationalism among the Indians and they used it to boycott British made merchandise in favor of home-made products. This act affected the British economy forcing the British government to reevaluate their interest in India. Gandhi attacked the Britain's where it hurt them the most, their pocketbook.

He was punished and imprisoned for his activism but refused to capitulate, knowing that his will and strength was directly connected to his people and any form of surrender would be seen as an acceptance of British rule. His beliefs impacted the people in such a way that they were able to unite and eventually see India freed from British control.

These are just a few great examples of people who came from modest backgrounds and were able to change the world. Others that come to mind are the son of a chief in South Africa, Nelson Mandela, fighting to end apartheid, Abraham Lincoln, Emiliano Zapata, William Wallace, St. Francis of Assisi and the list goes on and on. You can pick any continent, any country and anytime and there will always be someone who, in the face of injustice, rose from obscurity and changed their worlds. Why did I mention these in particular? Because they were humble people who were driven to make the world a better place, with no thought of personal gratification. In my opinion the two greatest of these were The Buddha and Jesus Christ who, while sharing their love and compassion with the world, impacted millions for generations. *"Love one another as I have loved you"*, the words spoken by Jesus are often referred to at the new commandment, it was one of the pillars of his message. Imagine how different history would have been or how much better humanity would be if we would have just listened to him? It's never too late to start. How about the Buddha who says, *"Radiate boundless love towards the entire world — above, below, and across — unhindered, without ill will, without enmity."* Wow, that's a lot of Love, can there really be too much Love? I don't believe so.

These great role models heavily impacted those around them, they all left the world a better place than when they arrived. I challenge you to do the same, not in so grand a scale but in your communities, schools and towns.

We all have the ability to positively impact our fellow human beings, some of us in a great way and others one at a time. Never underestimate your gifts, everyone has someone in their lives that looks up to them.

Start by helping someone be the best versions of themselves, be someone's hero.

"It is of no worth to be full of wisdom or vitality if we lack courage."-Dr. Pedro Albizu Campos. Attorney, Puerto Rico Civil Rights Activist & Patriot

WRITTEN ON THE WALL IN MOTHER TERESA'S HOME
FOR THE CHILDREN IN CALCUTTA

People are often unreasonable, irrational, and self-centered.
Forgive them anyway.

If you are kind, people may accuse you of selfish, ulterior motives.
Be kind anyway.

If you are successful, you will win some unfaithful friends and some
genuine enemies. Succeed anyway.

If you are honest and sincere people may deceive you.
Be honest and sincere anyway.

What you spend years creating, others could destroy
overnight. Create anyway.

If you find serenity and happiness, some may be jealous.
Be happy anyway.

The good you do today, will often be forgotten.
Do good anyway.

Give the best you have, and it will never be enough.
Give your best anyway

In the final analysis, it is between you and God.
It was never between you and them anyway.

A WARRIOR'S OBJECTIVE

TAKE-BUILD-GIVE. This is the formula that has always helped me prepare for and accomplish the objective. You can look at any objective as the goal or the mission. Prior to enacting the plan, focus on the final objective and determine if this is what you indeed want. I would always suggest that you write it down and leave it in a place where you can see it repeatedly. I'm not talking about the new year's resolution that everyone makes and only 2% keep, I'm talking about something much deeper and long lasting. These are your long-term goals. Visualize a positive outcome and see yourself in a post objective future, moving forward as if the mission was completed and successful.

First you start by absorbing, by consuming and taking. When others see you doing this, they might think you are being selfish and self-serving, they will fail to understand what you are planning and where you are going. You know that you will need to be ready, when the battle begins, and you make the decision to attack your goals, then the warrior that lives in you acts. I always think of the routine speech given to all of us on the onset of a flight by the flight attendant and how they remind everyone to put your mask on before you put on or help another with theirs. They understand that if you cannot help yourself first, you will not be available to help anyone else. Investing in yourself! Take in anything that will help fulfill your task. If you're focusing on improving your combatives skills then you must first start by being honest with yourself and taking a long hard look at your personal flaws. Only by doing this can you fill in those gaps and move to a higher level.

When you've taken the necessary steps to fulfill your objective, time to build. Build your team, build the program and build yourself. As I said earlier, invest heavily in yourself by taking in as much information as possible, but what's the point of all the learning, studying and preparing if you're never going to do anything with it? Sure, you might fail but, as we've discussed before, all warriors fail but that doesn't mean that they are not going to try. Time to act! Remember these words by the famous author and poet, Paulo Coelho, *"And, when you want something, all the universe conspires in helping you achieve it."*

When you've completed the next objective and, like a carpenter on steroids, built and fulfilled your dreams, then it's time to give back. If you're the crab in the barrel that managed to get out, you will probably think of a million reasons why you don't want to go or even look back but it's my belief that you should. Give back. Reach into that barrel and help another crab out. I know that this analogy gets overused, especially by me, but if it helped paint the picture of what I'm telling you to do and send you a clear message, so what? You could start by supporting a charity that you're passionate about, giving to your local food pantry, donating or speaking to support groups, etc. There are endless possibilities of how you can give back, and when you do, and you will, you will experience a powerful sense of joy and fulfillment knowing that your life, your dreams and all your achievements have helped others.

This is the good path, the warrior way and the right thing to do, it's a good karmic response to all you've received.

Have you established your objectives? Have you made goals and are you doing what needs to be done to see that they are accomplished? If you haven't, fine, get to it!

"Are you paralyzed with fear? That's a good sign. Fear is good. Like self-doubt, fear is an indicator. Fear tells us what we have to do. Remember one rule of thumb: the more scared we are of a work or calling, the more sure we can be that we have to do it."-Steven Pressfield, The War of Art: Winning the Inner Creative Battle

ENVISION WHAT YOU WILL BE

In the last topic we spoke about visualizing the objective completed. I just wanted to spend a little more time discussing this and the importance of this.

When I was young, I never tried to focus on where I was but where I was going. Some of you might say that this was not a very zen way to think, but I had a plan and I was always trying to work toward it. I wanted to be a cop, I wanted to be the type of person that people could count on for help and to be there to defend others when called upon. It was one of the reasons that I became involved in the martial arts in the first place, well, that and a mother who desperately wanted to keep me out of trouble.

Later, I entered the Air Force, not because I had any intention to fly but because they had a great police program and I could start doing police type work right away without going through any type of cadet training or waiting till I turned 21. When I left the military, the first job I took was a security position working at an AT&T facility. I was one of those guys that checks everyone's ID when they entered the building. Many would comment that I was always cheerful and would greet them with a smile, I guess they had become accustomed to others being rude and just plain grumpy. Finally, a lady asked me why I was always so happy when it seemed that all the security guards working always seemed to be upset and in a bad mood. I remember saying, "For me, this job is temporary, one day you'll come to work and I'll be gone." I had no problem keeping a smile on my face because I had a plan and this was all part of it, I knew the job was temporary, therefore I wasn't bothered by the day-to-day annoyances of it.

It's incredibly important to picture yourself doing that which you are attempting, to see yourself performing the mundane tasks associated with it and already enjoying the life that you are working towards.

Focus on where you want to be, what you're planning on doing to get there and finally, what you will do when you've arrived.

Whatever you ask for in prayer, believe that you have received it and it will be yours.
-Mark 11:24
Holy Bible

BE STRONG, BE THANKFUL, BE OF SERVICE

The three B's. There are certain things that should be done daily. We brush our teeth, shower, dress and check our weapon load, okay, the last one is just me. I like to focus on the 3 B's, Be Strong, Be Thankful and Be of Service.

Be Strong. In the first story at the beginning of this book I mentioned the importance of being strong, not just physically but mentally as well for yourself and for others. If you have not made an effort to make yourself strong, how do you expect to be there for others? How about defending your family or giving moral support during an emotionally charged crisis, you're of no use if you fall apart yourself. Do something every day that will help you become stronger. Train, workout and exercise your brain by reading. We all hope for the best but the day may come when we are forced to defend ourselves or a loved one, that is not the time to wish you had done more.

Be Thankful. Wake up in the morning and just give thanks for everything you have and all the blessings that you have received. Let God, the Universe or Wakan Tanka, the great Unknown know how much you appreciate everything in your life. Send that message out in prayer or good thoughts. This will immediately start your day on a positive note.

Can't find something to be grateful for? How about your family, your health, your job? Still can't think of anything? You might need to refocus on the first B.

Be of Service. Find a way to be of service, you can do this on a small scale or a big one. As warriors, we understand service, it's the duty we perform in order to assist, defend or elevate those in need. I always think of those that volunteer their time in order to improve someone's quality of life and in some cases actually save lives. A crisis intervention specialist who talks and safely resolves a hostile situation, an addiction sponsor who's there in a time of need to prevent a person from falling back into a toxic habit, or the coach who spends his free time keeping kids off the streets by making sure they are active and busy. Many of these people will never know how much they've impacted the lives of others. They do it because they want to, they're content to help. Their service is never forced, it's always given.

"Help the weak and vulnerable. Use your martial skills for the good of humanity."

Ip Man

Martial Arts Master & Teacher

WARRIOR OF THE LIGHT

"A Warrior knows that an angel and a devil are both competing for his sword hand.

The devil says: "You will weaken. You will not know exactly when. You are afraid."

The angel says: "You will weaken. You will not know exactly when. You are afraid."

The Warrior is surprised. Both the angel and the devil have said the same thing.

The devil continues: "Let me help you." And the angel says: "I will help you."

At that moment the Warrior understands the difference.

The words may be the same but these two allies are completely different.

And he chooses the angel's hand."

Paulo Coelho, Warrior of the Light

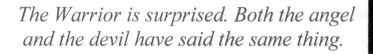

UNTAPPED POTENTIAL

I've had students tell me that they honestly feel that they were meant for greater things and that they believe that they should be doing more than what they are currently doing. I always agree with them, if you're having those feelings then they are probably true. Then I ask, "what are you doing to get there?" I'm almost always faced with a blank stare.

That's great that you feel that way but I sincerely hope that you're not just sitting back and waiting for the universe to take care of it all for you, you had better be doing something about it, God's too busy dealing with the issues of the world to do something for you that you can do for yourself. Don't be one of those people that read Rhonda Byrne's *The Secret* and are now expecting everything to come to you simply because you are envisioning the perfect positive outcome? That's a powerful little book but I think you're missing a major part of the recipe, the work required. Yes, you must absolutely get your hands dirty and start actively working towards your goals. What's your passion? What's the mission? Figure that out first, and then step by step move towards it.

There are times in your life that you may feel that you are on a good path and that there's nothing that you can't do wrong. Everything is working the way you want and bam! Something derailed your plans, something that was totally outside of your control. There have been plenty of times in my life when I thought that nothing could go wrong and something did. Murphy is a son of a b#@ch!

In 2016, I was struck by a car while helping my daughter with hers. The impact caused head trauma and brain injury; my wife would say that I had a brain injury long before the accident. An attempt was made to medivac me by helicopter to a hospital that had a trauma unit available that specialized in head injuries. Due to my being in and out of consciousness, I was only slightly aware of what was happening. During those times that I did regain consciousness, I would panic because I couldn't tell what was wrong with me since my head was strapped down and my entire body was immobilized.

As it turned out the helicopter was on another call and I would need to be transported by ambulance. I won't get into any more of the details suffice as to say that my life took a dramatic turn at that point. That day was the last day that I would work at the police department in a full capacity. It would take me approximately three months to walk without assistance and left me with poor balance and permanent hearing loss on my right side. I did not plan for these things to happen but I do remember thinking, now what? I needed a new plan, or at the very least modify the old one. The first thing I needed though was to get the hell out of the hospital. Every day, when the doctors would come in and see me, I would ask them how much longer would I be in the hospital. They explained to me all the reasons why I needed to be there longer than originally expected and that I might even have to be transferred to a physical therapy facility for long term recovery. All I heard was that I wasn't leaving anywhere anytime soon. Against the doctors wishes and with the help of my wife and brother, I signed myself out of the hospital. I strongly believed that if I was going to get better fast, it wasn't going to be there, turns out, I was right.

Andy Frisilla, a founder and co-owner of 1st Phorm Nutritional Supplements and creator of the 75 Hard program, often shares with the public an event that occurred to him at a time when his business was just starting out. While defending the honor of a friend of his who was the recipient of a racially charged remark, Frisilla was severely cut with a knife several times across the face. This event could have, and probably should have broken him, but, because he had a mission and remained focused and on point, he persevered and continued on his journey. I don't know the man but it seems to me that the events of that day, as horrific as they were, made him stronger. The reason I share Andy Frisella's story with you is because when I first heard it, it resonated with me, it touched me deeply, here was someone with no ill intent, fighting a bully and ending up getting scarred for life. Bad things can happen to anyone and they often do. When those bad times arrive, you must be ready, anticipate them and don't allow them to unbalance or break you, don't allow anything to stop you!

My accident sucked, it was obviously not a part of my plan, I had been knocked down but I knew that it wouldn't stop me. Through training and perseverance, I got back to the Dojang in record time. I was no longer a police officer but, considering the circumstances and how badly things could have turned out, I was lucky to be alive.

Keep moving forward, every day do a little something that gets you closer to your dreams and keeps you on your path. If you truly believe you were meant for bigger things, that you have untapped potential, then do something great. I look forward to hearing your story someday.

"Life is never made unbearable by circumstances,
but only by lack of meaning and purpose."

-Viktor Frankl

Author, Holocaust Survivor

AVOID THE CURB

When I first learned to ride a motorcycle and attempt to properly negotiate the turns, the friend that was teaching me would say, "Don't stare at the curb, if you focus on it, that's where you'll go." He would go on to further explain that it's important to concentrate on where you want the bike to go and not where you absolutely did not want to be. I remember thinking how similar  that is to regular life. How many people spend their lives focused on the "curbs" and, because of that, drive right into them.

In your life you will hear people tell you don't do this or that because something bad might happen, you might fail or get hurt, they might even give you examples. They have their own fears and they want you to share them, after all, by nature we are tribal and want people to think like we do. But you must keep in mind that those people, although they might not wish you harm, have spent their lives staring at "curbs" and can't focus on anything else. To achieve your personal goal, you're going to have to push those boundaries and go where others fear, remember the old cliché? If it was easy, everyone would do it.

Good things are never easy, the best things, the things that last the longest and matter the most have always required hard work. There is nothing like that feeling of satisfaction you get when you completed something of value. Remember how I told you that life is like the Dojo? If it's done correctly, it's not easy, you will be hurt, humbled, and often feel that your own abilities are inadequate in comparison to others but that does not mean you will spend time focusing on that. You must remember that the possibility of something negative happening is always there, so what? Those who are unrealistic about their training and life in general will always quit when dealing with adversity, they remember all the times they were told, "Why are you doing that? You're going to get hurt", then when it does happen, they say, "Ahh, they were right, I got hurt." Of course, you got hurt! You had your eyes on the "curb". You spent all that time focusing on the negative and then have the nerve to actually be shocked when it happens.

No matter what I do or how much time passes, I'll always remember my motorcycle training all those years ago and learning how to control that bike. After all that time, the one training tip that is still present and I will never forget, don't focus on the curb.

"Your life is controlled by what you focus on".
-Tony Robbins

YOU'RE NOT INJURED, YOU'RE HURT

This question comes up often. I'm frequently asked, "what's the difference between being hurt and being injured?"

There is a difference. Being hurt is something along the lines of minor scrapes and bruises, getting punched in the face, etc., those you can shake off and be back in training for the next class. You feel the pain but it doesn't incapacitate you and leave you unable to function or train.

Being injured can be much longer lasting and requires some recovery time. A broken bone, twisted ankle or pulled tendon are examples of these.

Whether or not the injury occurred during training, I always encourage students to continue attending class, training in a "light duty" capacity or assist other students by coaching and helping to run drills. Being present keeps them active and part of the group and helps them speed up their recovery. Bad habits are much easier to develop than good ones, you don't want them to become accustomed to not training, and generally speaking, most will be glad to still be part of the training process.

Now, there are always those individuals that are looking for a way out. Instead of just slowing down when things got difficult, they've lost their original drive and have forgotten why they started in the first place. When they are injured or hurt, I know that when they walk out the door, they are never coming back. They have given in to the little voice inside that says, "this is too hard for you, you shouldn't be doing this anyway."

All goals and dreams are the same, on the journey you may be "injured or hurt", metaphorically speaking, trying to achieve something great, if you are quick to abandon those goals, then how badly did you really want it?

Everybody comes to a point in their life when they want to quit. But it's what you do at that moment that determines who you are. -David Goggins

RESPECT

The dictionary defines the term respect as a "a feeling of deep admiration for someone or something elicited by their abilities, qualities, or achievements." Most people want to be respected, songs have been written on the subject and wars started by its denial.

The way a person is treated, no matter who they are, what race they belong, or their social or economic status, is very important and should never be denied.

But let's step back and take a minute to revisit the definition of the word, RESPECT. According to the definition, it states, "deep admiration for someone or something elicited by their abilities, qualities, or achievements." So that brings up the point, should respect be given or earned? What if someone hasn't seen your qualities or  achievements? What if you have no special abilities, have you earned respect? Many will demand respect but do nothing to earn it, they feel it is a right and owed to them. What do you think? What about those that demand respect but refuse to give it to others? Or, those people that only show respect to the ones they deem worthy because of their race or economic status? Should they be respected?

For my part, I will always treat others the way that I would expect someone to treat me or my loved ones. I believe that all human beings deserve that level of respect and I try my best to give it to them, but as expected, that may change depending on their behavior.

Being disrespectful and rude to others yet demanding it of yourself is the sign of an entitled child. I have seen so much of that these days that I'm grateful when I see the martial arts students training and working together in a polite and helpful manner. It's one of the best things about the fighting arts that those that are not familiar with them forget or don't know about. Teaching such things as manners, respect, empathy, honor, loyalty and understanding is something that I feel modern society has chosen to disregard. The warrior way is more than just fighting, it's a way of living.

"I respect myself and insist upon it from everybody. And because I do it, I then respect everybody, too".
-Maya Angelou
Poet & Activist

90 SECONDS

Recently I had a discussion with my son about the importance of getting things done and how when we procrastinate not only does it delay our goals, it shows our lack of desire and determination to follow-through. Now, I know that we all put things off, especially those things that we really hate to do. I'm due for a colonoscopy, not in any hurry to do that, but I know that it needs to get done, ugh. But for the sake of this conversation, I'm going to be talking about all the little things that have that annoying habit of building up. My son told me that every time he gets confronted with a situation where he thinks that he would like to put it off for later that day or the next day, he asks himself if getting it done will take less than ninety seconds. If it does, then there is absolutely no reason not to get it done now.

You would be amazed how many little things that we put off that can simply be done in less than 90 seconds. I will write in my journal the little things that need to be done that day and then put a little check mark next to it when it's completed, if it doesn't get done then I have to rewrite it for the next day and, because I hate rewrites, I will do everything I can to make sure that it gets done. For me, that's enough incentive, this includes my workouts.

It doesn't seem like a lot can get accomplished in such a short amount of time, but all those little things have the habit of piling up, big things get accomplished by doing the little things, plain and simple.

Having a hard time getting past all the procrastination? Rather than focusing on the 90 seconds that it takes to get the task completed, you might start first by refocusing on your daily goal.

Remember this, lack of passion causes a lack of desire, lack of desire causes a lack of motivation, lack of motivation results in Mission Failure!

90 Seconds. Remember, use this rule to help you get things done, eliminate procrastination and complete your goals.

"Procrastination is the grave in which opportunity is buried." -
Author Unknown

WATER

I'm not gonna spend a lot of time on this one, Bruce Lee covered this subject pretty well, a copy of his words on the subject can be found at the end of this article and it is actually hanging on my office wall at The Defense Training Institute.

I've been hearing about the principle of water long before I heard Bruce Lee's *Be Water* quote. Many who train in the martial arts actually use the philosophy of Water as a guideline for their movements and forms, this is most likely the reason that his words resonate with so many martial artists.

But, in my opinion, people who discuss Bruce Lee's *Be Water* quote tend to focus on the act of absorbing and redirecting an attack and ignore or gloss over the ending where he states that "Water can drip or it can crash." So, let's talk about that. What's the point of focusing on the "soft" parts of the martial arts if we ignore the "hard"? Let's remember that water, like all elements, is a very Yin Yang force. It can be absorbed and redirected but it can additionally overwhelm before it flows it impacts. Absorbing your opponent's attack sounds good in principle but only until you are faced with overwhelming odds like a bigger and more powerful opponent. Redirecting an opponent's power, strength and energy requires an extraordinary amount of training. While I'm all for controlling your adversary, it's important to be realistic. Sometimes your opponent is just bigger, stronger, faster or younger than you. When defending against a skilled fighter, it is necessary for you to master the art of striking as well as

128

becoming equally proficient at tactically targeting the right locations, the strike points, to cause maximum damage. This is one of the core elements of Guazabara, not only with a blunt weapon but also with a knife and free hand. Sometimes you don't get multiple chances and a prolonged fight is not an option, like water, you must crash and overwhelm your opponent, refusing to allow them the opportunity to adjust and anticipate your actions. The philosophy of water takes on a whole new meaning when you think of it in these terms. We learn a great deal by watching and being guided by nature, keep in mind the power of water and the damage that it can do.

Let's now step away from the martial arts and talk about life in general. You've heard me say several times that the training hall can be similar to life and that many of the lessons learned in the dojo can be used in our daily lives. That applies here as well. While it is important to never back down from an adversary, sometimes we must find a way to absorb their attacks and redirect them in a way that is advantageous. When all attempts at defense have been exhausted and your opponent continues to push the matter, you may be forced to "draw a line" and push back.

Many tools can be utilized to fix a problem, but it's important to remember that when all else fails, a hammer may be your final option, so it's good to have one in your tool box.

Be Water

"You must be shapeless, formless, like water. When you pour water in a cup, it becomes the cup. When you pour water in a bottle, it becomes the bottle. When you pour water in a teapot, it becomes the teapot. Water can drip and it can crash. Become like water my friend." -Bruce Lee

FAITH AND THE WAY OF THE SWORD

People can get very uncomfortable when the subject of faith, religion and personal beliefs comes up, it's like walking on broken glass. I debated with myself whether or not I should add this topic to Martial Thought but, as I stated in the beginning of the book, these are all topics that originated from conversations that I've had with my students over the past twenty years and I thought it important not to exclude this.

For many, this subject can be very personal and their relationship with the Almighty is a private matter. It's difficult to think of a topic that can elicit higher levels of emotion more than religion. Yet, I would be remiss if I didn't say something on the matter since it's such an important part of the warrior way of thinking and lifestyle.

I grew up in a strong Catholic home, and like so many that may have been raised in the same way, I grew up to question so much of what I had been taught. I think this is something that a lot of people go through and probably very normal. There are so many rules that seemed designed to benefit only a few at the expense of the many. From my point of view, history had chosen to use something that was beautifully simple and made it complicated to control the masses. The words of a simple carpenter over 2000 years ago should resonate with everyone regardless of their personal beliefs, "Love one another as I have loved you." What can be more perfect than that? 500 years ago, the Europeans arrived on the shores of the Caribbean islands, forcing their beliefs on my ancestors. They spoke of love and eternal salvation, but good words mean very little when they come from the mouths of hate, bigotry, judgement and intolerance. Those first people were one in a long line of cultures and traditions throughout the world forced to capitulate to the ways of others in the name of "love". If they had just come and shared true love and understanding, imagine the world we would live in now? The first people of the Americas, the Taino, Caribe and Maya would have been more accepting of a religion that was backed by good and honorable actions.

Why do I share this with you now? Because it's a starting point for a bigger conversation. I remember reading the words of Black Elk, a Lakota Holy Man, who, after reading the New Testament said that he really liked Jesus. He went on to say that the "people" (referring to the Lakota), followed the ways of Jesus more than the Christians did. The Lakota go into the wilderness to pray, they treat each other with respect and care for those in need, isn't this what Jesus did? Wise words from this native holy man. He could not understand why native people were treated so poorly when they lived a life similar to the one that Jesus did. You know what? I don't either. How do you answer that question? I use the Americas as an example but this scenario was played out in cultures all over the world, people were forced to believe in the ways of others.

All this made me question absolutely everything that I had been taught. How can I believe something that was forced upon my ancestors through persecution and pain? The same treatment that Christians had received in the first century they proceeded to "dish out" to others.

 We can try to rewrite or retell history, but it is what it is and there is no changing the good with the bad. Through a great deal of soul searching, I stopped and thought, how would Jesus feel? How would he feel about his message being used to create fear, to conquer, to kill and to hate? I'm sure he was heartbroken! I think of his humanity and believe that he would have been in a great deal of pain, that he felt every death and mourned for the loss of life. This was not what he wanted. He taught us the Lord's Prayer in an effort to eliminate the "middleman" and pray directly to God, but through the folly of man, control had to be established and his words were used to create pain and suffering.

This forced me to question everything, even his divinity. But one story resonated with me more than any other, this was the story of Pentecost. The Acts of the Apostles is a very powerful chapter in the New Testament, one that is sometimes overlooked. Imagine yourself in a situation where you are being hunted, your teacher and mentor was tortured and publicly executed. You're living with the fear that if you are captured, the same will happen to you. If you can't picture this or still don't understand a little of what they were going through, then you've never been in a position where you were truly afraid for your life.

Fearing for their lives and those of their loved ones, should their connection to Jesus be discovered, the disciples went into hiding. Then one day, their fear was gone. They ALL began preaching and spreading the gospel of Jesus. What changed? What happened on that day that made them all put aside their fears and go in public to share their beliefs regardless of the consequences? Truthfully, they could have easily just blended into society and put it all behind them, but they chose instead to step out of the shadows and show the world their faith knowing full well that they would share the same fate as their mentor.

As a student of human nature, I have to believe that the odds of all these people simultaneously setting their fears aside had to be astronomical, something powerful happened, something so strong that the fear of torture and death did not stop them, something like Faith.

Faith is about the belief in something greater and more powerful than yourself. Believe what you will, for me, this story gives me the hope that the words spoken by that small town Jewish rabbi over two thousand years ago still has relevance.

So, how does someone like me balance faith and the need to study, train and teach violence? Defense. Defense of ourselves and others. If you want to be there for others then prepare for tomorrow's battle, if it never comes to that, then consider yourself blessed and if it does, you'll be ready.

Watch, stand fast in the faith, be brave, be strong.
1 Corinthians 16:13

About the Author

 Edgardo Pérez is a military veteran with 30 years of police service and over 40 years of study in the martial arts. He is a Hand-to-Hand Combat Instructor that holds an 8th Degree Master's Rank in Hapkido and the founder of the JunSa Kwan Hapkido system as well as the founder of Guazabara Machete, Knife & Stick Fighting, a full instructor in Largo Mano Filipino Kali-Eskrima, Police Combatives and student of Brazilian Jiu-Jitsu.

In 1979 Master Perez began his formal martial arts training in Hapkido under the tutelage of the Fowler Brothers in Aurora, Il. He later continued his training in South Korea under Grandmaster Yu Chong Su (Chong Su Kwan Hapkido & Kumdo).

For the past 40 years Perez has continued to train in Hapkido while teaching local, county and state police personnel in police combatives. In 1998 Perez founded the Martial Arts Gang Intervention Club (MAGIC) and the Defense Training Institute.

In 2014 Perez founded "Kicking for Heroes", a yearly Kick-a-thon raising money for our police, military and children in need. Through the generosity of "kickers", their parents and all our sponsors, "Kicking for Heroes" has donated just over $26,000 to various charities in the last 5 years.

In 2016 Perez retired after serving as a patrol officer, an undercover narcotic operative with the FBI and Illinois State Police, a sergeant, detective sergeant, Field Training Officer, Defensive Tactics Instructor, Gang Specialist and DEA Undercover Operative and Consultant, Perez retired.

He currently serves as the Defensive Tactics Coordinator for the Kane County Sheriff's Office in Kane County Illinois as well as the Chief Instructor/Owner of The Defense Training Institute.

Contact: www.defensetraininginstitute.net
Instagram: @coacheddieperez

All that has been, will be.
All that will be, has been.
Every ending is just a beginning.
-Edgardo Perez

CPSIA information can be obtained
at www.ICGtesting.com
Printed in the USA
BVHW011808270621
610598BV00008B/305